BARITONE UKULELE FRETBOARD ROADMAPS

THE ESSENTIAL PATTERNS THAT ALL THE PROS KNOW AND USE

BY FRED SOKOLOW

Speed • Pitch • Balance • Loop

To access audio visit:
www.halleonard.com/mylibrary
Enter Code
3555-3548-7148-1734

The Recording
Baritone Uke, Other Stringed Instruments, and Vocals—Fred Sokolow
Sound Engineer and Other Instruments—Michael Monagan
Recorded at Sossity Sound

Editorial assistance by Ronny S. Schiff

ISBN 978-1-4950-7639-8

7777 W. BLUEMOUND RD. P.O. BOX 13819 MILWAUKEE, WI 53213

In Australia Contact:
Hal Leonard Australia Pty. Ltd.
4 Lentara Court
Cheltenham, Victoria, 3192 Australia
Email: ausadmin@halleonard.com.au

Visit Hal Leonard Online at
www.halleonard.com

CONTENTS

INTRODUCTION

The ukulele renaissance of recent years has brought new attention to the uke's cousins: the bass uke and the baritone uke. Though the bass uke is a recent invention, baritone ukes have been around since the late '40s, when stringed instrument makers John and Joseph Favilla started manufacturing them. Arthur Godfrey helped popularize the "bari," and several music manufacturers began building them.

Some music teachers used the baritone as a stepping stone to guitar because it's easier to play than its six-stringed relative. But many of today's uke and guitar players find that the baritone has its own personality and charm.

Whether you're a rank beginner or already play the baritone uke, this book will give you the skills and techniques you need to take it as far as you want to go. Accomplished baritone uke players can strum the bari to accompany singing, but they can also ad-lib hot solos and play lead or backup in any key—all over the fretboard. They can play songs of nearly any genre: Hawaiian, Tin Pan Alley, folk, Dixieland, country, blues, rock, or jazz.

There are moveable patterns on the bari fretboard that make it easy to do these things. The pros are aware of these "fretboard roadmaps," even if they don't read music. Whether you want to jam with other players or be an accomplished solo player, *this is essential knowledge.*

You need the fretboard roadmaps if...

- You don't know how to play in every key.

- Your baritone fretboard beyond the 5th fret is uncharted territory.

- Certain chords are mysterious and unknown.

- You've memorized a few tunes on the bari, but you don't know how to make up your own arrangements or improvise.

- You can strum a tune to back up your singing, but you can't play an instrumental solo.

Read on, and many mysteries will be explained. If you're serious about playing the baritone, the pages that follow can shed light and save you a great deal of time.

Good luck,

Fred Sokolow

THE RECORDING AND THE PRACTICE TRACKS

To access the audio examples that accompany this book, simply visit **www.halleonard.com/mylibrary** and enter the code found on page 1. There, you can download or stream all of the audio tracks.

All the licks, riffs, and tunes in this book are played on the audio tracks. Also included are four Practice Tracks that are mixed so that the bari is on one side of your audio player and the backup band is on the other.

Each track illustrates one or more *Roadmap* concepts, such as bluesy soloing or circle-of-fifths chord progressions. Plus, you can tune out the baritone track and practice by playing along with the backup tracks.

PRELIMINARIES

TUNING

The baritone is tuned D–G–B–E, starting from the heaviest (4th) string. It's the same as the top four strings of a guitar.

Use Track 1 to tune, so you can play along with the songs and exercises. If the 4th string is tuned to any tuning device, you can also use the string-to-string method described below to tune the other strings:

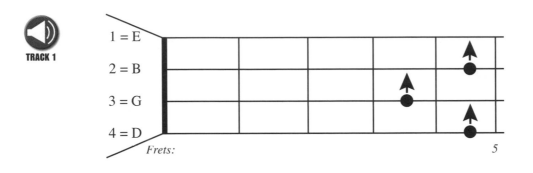

As the above diagram shows, once you've tuned the open 4th (D) string, you can:
- Tune the 3rd (G) string by matching it to the 4th string/5th fret,
- Tune the 2nd (B) string by matching it to the 3rd string/4th fret,
- Tune the 1st (E) string by matching it to the 2nd string/5th fret.

CONVERSIONS FOR UKE AND GUITAR PLAYERS

If you play guitar or uke, you're way ahead of the game.

Guitar Players: You can use the same chords, scales, and licks you already play on guitar; *you just have to make the adjustment to four strings instead of six.* Those bass strings (the 6th and 5th) are gone!

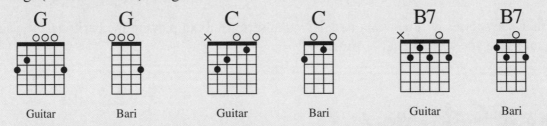

Uke Players: You can also use the chords, scales, and licks you learned for uke, but the names of the chords and notes are a 5th higher (if you don't know what "a 5th higher" means, it's explained in **ROADMAP #2: THE MAJOR SCALE**).

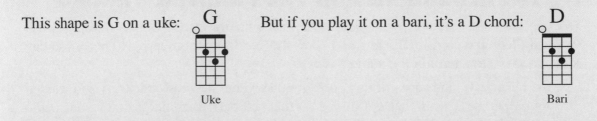

Here's another way to look at it: to translate from uke to bari, think up a 4th. In other words, if you need to play a D chord on bari, play the uke shape for a G chord (G is a 4th above D).

STRUMMING PATTERNS

Most people strum the baritone with their fingers, while some use a felt pick. Either way, the movement comes from your wrist, not your arm.

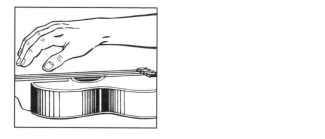

Some use their thumb for downstrokes and index finger for upstrokes; others use the index finger for both up and downstrokes. Any variation that works for you is fine. If you choose to use a pick, hold it like this:

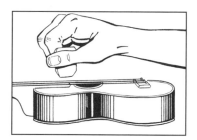

The strums on Tracks 2, 3, 4, and 5 are played on open (unfretted) strings—a G6 chord.

BASIC STRUM, 4/4 TIME
1. Strum down with the thumb, index finger, or pick.
2. Then strum up with the index finger or pick.
3. Repeat Steps 1 and 2 three more times to create this 4/4 rhythm:

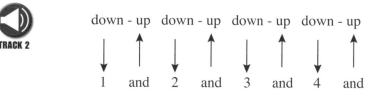

Listen to the track to hear how you can create a shuffle beat or a straight-eighths rock groove with this simple strum, just by changing your emphasis. (The shuffle beat, similar to a swing beat, has a skipping rhythm, as in "Crazy Little Thing Called Love," "Kansas City," or "Yellow Submarine." In the straight-eighths feel, the beat is more evenly divided, as in "[I Can't Get No] Satisfaction," "Beat It," or "Proud Mary.")

BASIC STRUM, VARIATION 1

Here's one of many possible variations of the basic strum: leave out the first "and." In other words…
1. Strum down with the thumb, index finger, or pick.
2. Strum down again with thumb, index, or pick.
3. Strum up with the index finger or pick.
4. Repeat Steps 2 and 3 two more times.

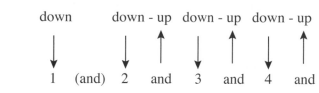

BASIC STRUM, VARIATION 2

One more variation: use the previous strum pattern but leave out the third downstroke.

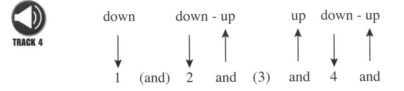

WALTZ STRUM, 3/4 TIME

Here's a strum in 3/4 time:
1. Strum down with the thumb, index finger, or pick.
2. Strum down with the thumb, index finger, or pick.
3. Strum up with the index finger or pick.
4. Strum down with the thumb, index finger, or pick.
5. Strum up with the index finger or pick.

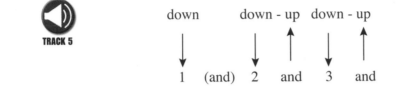

PICKING PATTERNS

Some players fingerpick the bari. They use the thumb, index, and middle finger—sometimes the ring finger.

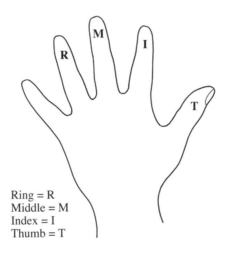

Ring = R
Middle = M
Index = I
Thumb = T

Here are some typical picking patterns:

FIRST-POSITION CHORDS

Here are some basic chords. The numbers indicate fret-hand fingerings. Strum all four strings for each chord.

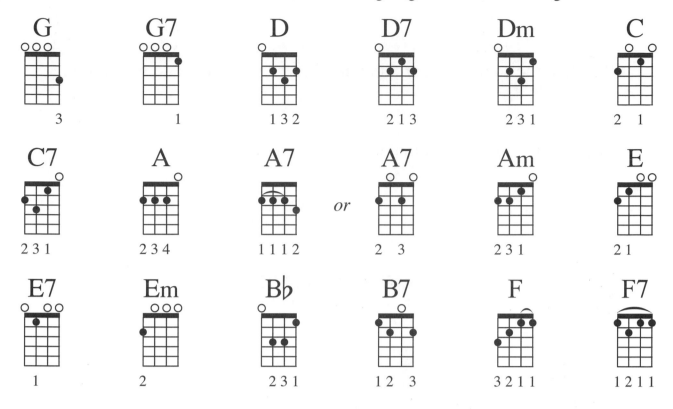

STRUMMING SOME SIMPLE TUNES

The following tunes will give you a chance to practice chord changes, the strums, and the picking patterns. Listen to each song before you start playing. Play each one as slowly as you need to in order to keep the rhythm smooth and steady. As soon as you can, play along with the recording.

 TRACK 7

SLOOP JOHN B.

Use the strum from Track 4, a variation of the 4/4 strum.

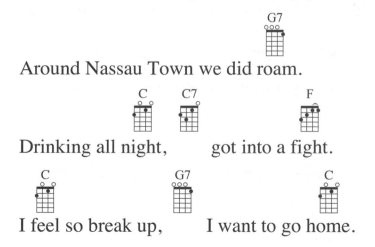

We come on the Sloop John B., my grandfather and me.

Around Nassau Town we did roam.

Drinking all night,   got into a fight.

I feel so break up,   I want to go home.

WHEN THE SAINTS GO MARCHING IN

TRACK 8

Use the strum from Track 3, a variation of the basic 4/4 strum.

G   D7

Oh, when the saints go marching in, oh, when the saints go marching in.

G   C   G   D7   G

Oh, Lord, I want to be in that number when the saints go marching in.

AMAZING GRACE

TRACK 9

Use the waltz strum from Track 5.

D   G   D   A7

Amazing grace, how sweet the sound that saved a wretch like me.

D   D7   G   D   A7   D

I once was lost but now I'm found, was blind but now I see.

GAMBLER'S BLUES

TRACK 10

Use the basic 4/4 strum from Track 2.

Am   E7   Am   Dm   Am

I was down in old Joe's barroom, at the corner of the square.

E7   Am   F   E   Am

The drinks were served as usual, and the usual crowd was there.

8

NOTES ON THE FRETBOARD

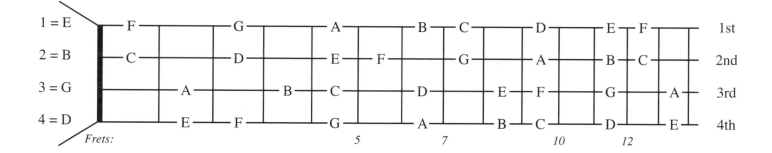

WHY? Knowing where the notes are located will help you find chords and scales up and down the neck. It will help you alter and understand chords (e.g., *Why is this chord minor instead of major? How do I flat the 7th in this chord?*). It's the first step toward understanding music.

You don't have to memorize every note on the fretboard! But if you learn the open-string notes and follow through with some of the suggestions below, you'll start to learn the notes in the first several frets, and the rest of the notes will follow eventually.

WHAT? The notes get higher in pitch as you go up the alphabet and up the fretboard.

A whole step is two frets, and a half step is one fret.

Sharps are one fret higher: 2nd string/1st fret = C, so 2nd string/2nd fret = C♯.

Flats are one fret lower: 3rd string/2nd fret = A, so 3rd string/1st fret = A♭.

HOW? The bari is tuned **D–G–B–E** (from 4th to 1st string). Start by learning these notes!

Fretboard markings help. Most baris have fretboard inlays or marks on the neck indicating the 5th, 7th, 10th, and 12th frets. Become aware of these signposts.

DO IT! Learn other notes in reference to the notes you already know.

The notes at the 2nd fret are a whole step higher than the open-string (unfretted) **notes.** The 3rd string/open (unfretted) = G, so 3rd string/2nd fret = A.

Everything starts over at the 12th fret. The open 1st string is E, so the 1st string/12th fret is also E.

You already know some notes from the string-to-string tuning method (from the Preliminaries section): the 4th string/5th fret = G, 3rd string/4th fret = B, and 2nd string/5th fret = E.

Learn the notes on the 1st string, and you'll also know the 4th-string notes:

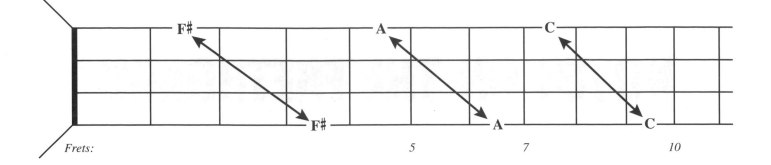

The 3rd string, three frets below the 1st string, is the same note an octave lower.

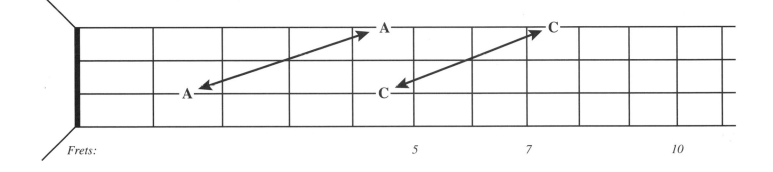

The 4th string, three frets below the 2nd string, is the same note an octave lower.

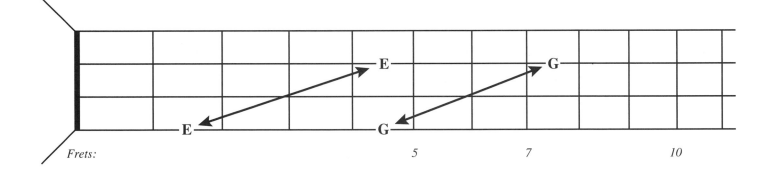

SUMMING UP—NOW YOU KNOW...

1. The location of the notes on the fretboard and some shortcuts to memorizing them.

2. The meanings of these musical terms:

   a) Whole Step

   b) Half Step

   c) Sharp (♯)

   d) Flat (♭)

THE MAJOR SCALE

C Major Scale

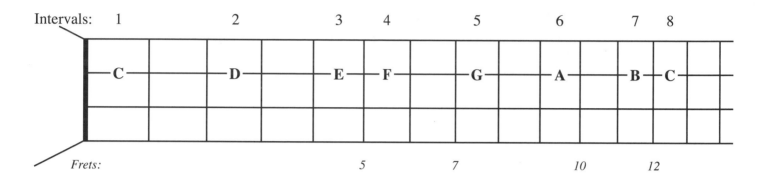

WHY? To understand music and to communicate with other players, you need to know about the major scale. The major scale is a ruler that helps you measure distances between notes and chords. Knowing the major scale will help you understand and talk about chord construction, scales, and chord relationships.

WHAT? **The major scale is the "Do-Re-Mi" scale you have heard all your life.** Countless familiar tunes are composed of notes from this scale.

Intervals **are distances between notes.** The intervals of the major scale are used to describe these distances. For example, E is the third note of the C major scale, and it is four frets above C (see above). This distance is called a *3rd*. Similarly, A is a 3rd above F, and C♯ is a 3rd above A. On the baritone, a 3rd is always the distance of four frets.

HOW? **Every major scale has the same interval pattern of whole and half steps:**

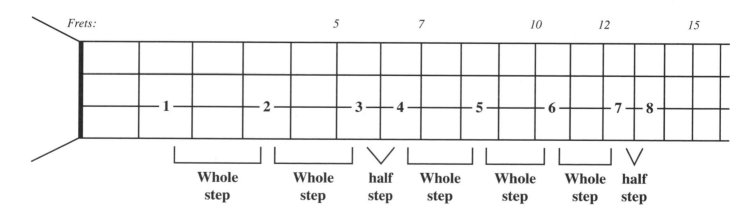

In other words, the major scale ascends by whole steps (two frets at a time) with two exceptions: there is a half step (one fret) from the third to the fourth note and from the seventh to the eighth note. It's helpful to think of intervals in terms of frets (e.g., going up a 3rd is the same as going up four frets).

Intervals can extend above the octave. They correspond to lower intervals:

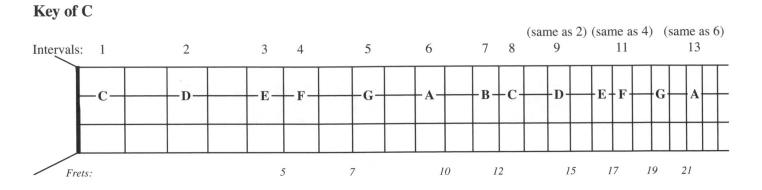

Key of C

| | (same as 2) | (same as 4) | (same as 6) |

Intervals: 1   2   3   4   5   6   7 8   9   11   13

C — D — E — F — G — A — B — C — D — E — F — G — A

Frets: 5   7   10   12   15   17   19   21

DO IT! **Learn the major scale intervals** by playing any note and finding the note that is a 3rd higher, a 4th higher, a 5th higher, etc.

SUMMING UP—NOW YOU KNOW...

The intervals of the major scale and the number of frets that make up each interval.

THE MOVEABLE D FORMATION AND ITS VARIATIONS

E Chords:

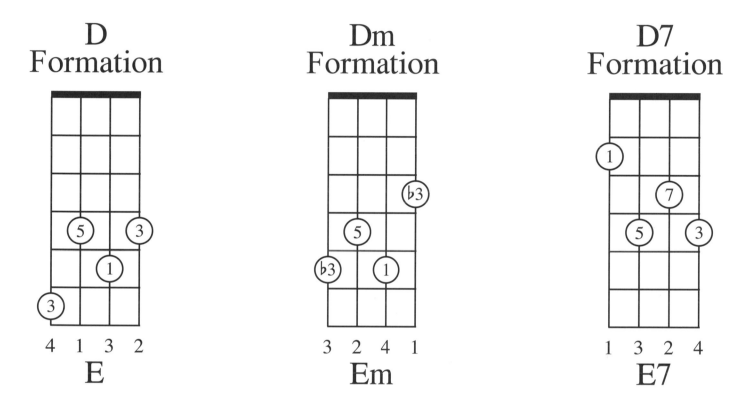

D Formation

Dm Formation

D7 Formation

E

Em

E7

WHY? **ROADMAPS #3, 4, and 5 will help you build a full chord vocabulary.** These three chapters have all the chords you'll need to play any song. And if you read on, you'll understand how the chords are constructed, which makes learning them much easier.

Think of this chapter as a *chord dictionary* that has the added bonus of explaining how each chord is built and showing its intervals. You won't have to memorize hundreds of random shapes, because each chord shape will have some meaning and will be similar to a chord you already know.

WHAT? A *chord* is a group of three or more notes played simultaneously.

A *moveable chord* can be played all over the fretboard. It contains no open (unfretted) strings.

The *root* is the note that gives a chord its name.

There are three types of chords: major, minor, and seventh chords. Each type has a distinct sound that you will come to recognize. Each chord type is constructed by combining specific notes:

- **Major chords consist of a root, 3rd, and 5th.** For example, D major is comprised of the first, third, and fifth notes of the D major scale: D, F♯, and A.

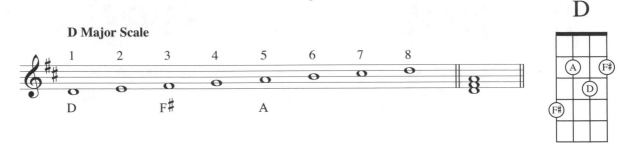

- **Minor chords consist of a root, ♭3rd, and 5th: Dm = D, F, and A.**

- **Seventh chords consist of a root, 3rd, 5th, and ♭7th: D7 = D, F♯, A, and C.**

In **ROADMAP #3,** the intervals of the D, Dm, and D7 formations are indicated by the circled numbers.

The D formation is so named because it's a moveable version of the first-position D chord. You don't have to fret the 4th string in the first-position D chord, but it must be fretted to make the chord formation moveable. If you move it up a fret, with all four strings fretted, it's a D♯ (or E♭) chord.

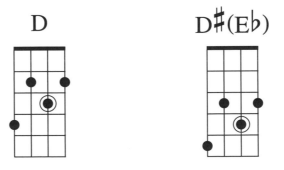

Wherever you play the D formation on the fretboard, *it's always a moveable chord*, and *the 2nd string is always the root*.

The three D formations of **ROADMAP #3** (D formation, Dm formation, and D7 formation) are "up two frets," so they are E, Em, and E7 chords.

Most people prefer to play the moveable D formation as a barred chord:

HOW?

The 2nd string is the root of the D and Dm formations. If you know the notes on the 2nd string, you can play these chord formations all over the fretboard and identify them by that string. In the diagrams below, the number to the right of the grid shows the fret number of your first (index) finger.

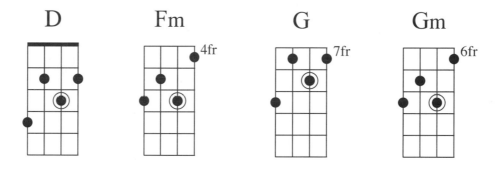

The 4th string is the root of the D7 formation. If you know the notes on the 4th string, you can play seventh chords all over the fretboard and identify them by that string.

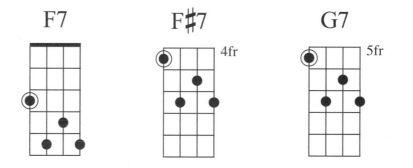

There are many ways to vary major, minor, or seventh chords to make them more colorful without changing their basic identity. For example, D major can be Dmaj7, D6, Dadd9, etc.

Many of these subtle chord variations resemble the basic major, minor, and seventh chord shapes—with one note added, or one note flatted or sharped.

DO IT!

Play the moveable D, Dm, and D7 formations all over the fretboard and name them.

Compare every new chord you learn to a basic chord you already know. Every small chord grid below is a variation of a basic chord formation.

Here are the most-played variations of the D, Dm, and D7 formations. Play them and compare each formation to the larger grid to the left—the chord from which it is derived. For consistency, all the forms are written as E chords.

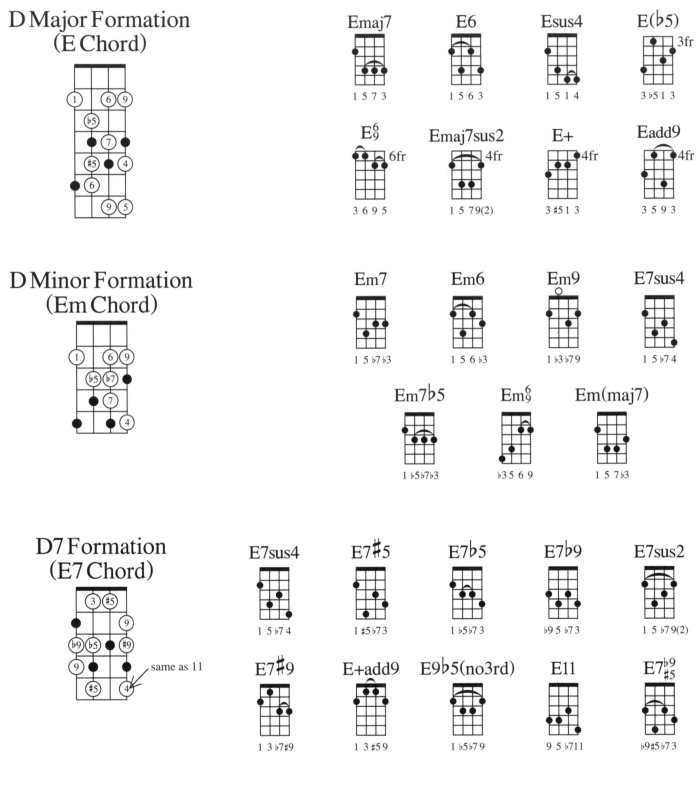

D Major Formation (E Chord)

Emaj7
1 5 7 3

E6
1 5 6 3

Esus4
1 5 1 4

E(♭5) 3fr
3 ♭5 1 3

E⁶₉ 6fr
3 6 9 5

Emaj7sus2 4fr
1 5 7 9(2)

E+ 4fr
3 #5 1 3

Eadd9 4fr
3 5 9 3

D Minor Formation (Em Chord)

Em7
1 5 ♭7 ♭3

Em6
1 5 6 ♭3

Em9
1 ♭3 ♭7 9

E7sus4
1 5 ♭7 4

Em7♭5
1 ♭5 ♭7 ♭3

Em⁶₉
♭3 5 6 9

Em(maj7)
1 5 7 ♭3

D7 Formation (E7 Chord)

E7sus4
1 5 ♭7 4

E7#5
1 #5 ♭7 3

E7♭5
1 ♭5 ♭7 3

E7♭9
♭9 5 ♭7 3

E7sus2
1 5 ♭7 9(2)

E7#9
1 3 ♭7 #9

E+add9
1 3 #5 9

E9♭5(no3rd)
1 ♭5 ♭7 9

E11
9 5 ♭7 11

E7♭9#5
♭9 #5 ♭7 3

same as 11

Here's another useful D7 formation:

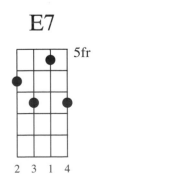

E7 5fr
2 3 1 4

E7 5fr

It lends itself to these variations:

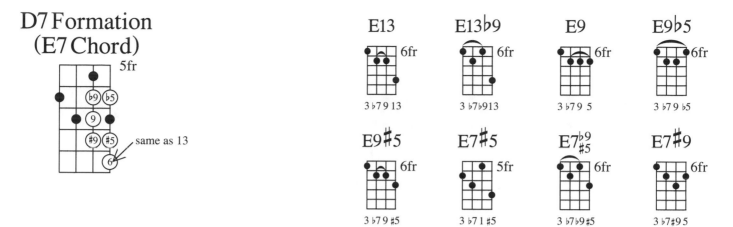

D7 Formation
(E7 Chord)

E13   E13♭9   E9   E9♭5

E9♯5   E7♯5   E7♭9♯5   E7♯9

DIMINISHED SEVENTH

The diminished seventh chord formula is 1–♭3–♭5–♭♭7. (The ♭♭7 note is the same note as the 6th.) A diminished chord is like a seventh chord with everything flatted but the root. Diminished chords repeat every three frets. The following are all E diminished chords ("°" is the symbol for diminished):

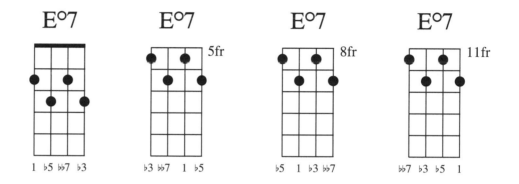

E°7   E°7   E°7   E°7

A diminished chord can be named by any of its four notes. For example, D°7 can also be called F°7, A♭°7, or B°7, depending on the context in which it occurs.

SUMMING UP—NOW YOU KNOW...

1. Four moveable D formations (major, minor, and two sevenths) and how to play them all over the fretboard.

2. The formulas for major, minor, seventh, and diminished seventh chords and how to play them using moveable formations.

3. How to vary the moveable major, minor, and seventh chords to play dozens of chord types: minor sevenths, sixths, major sevenths, etc.

4. The meaning of these musical terms:
   a) Chord
   b) Moveable Chord
   c) Root

THE MOVEABLE F FORMATION AND ITS VARIATIONS

G Chords:

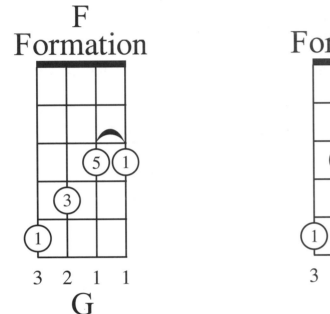

F
Formation

5 1

3

1

3 2 1 1

G

Fm
Formation

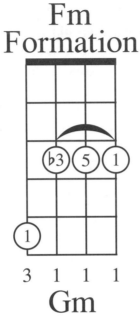

♭3 5 1

1

3 1 1 1

Gm

F7
Formation

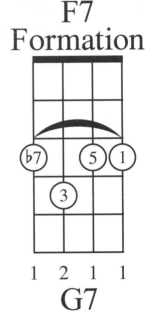

♭7   5 1

3

1 2 1 1

G7

WHY? The three F formations of **ROADMAP #4** will help you learn another entire set of moveable chords.

WHAT? **The F formation is so named because it's a moveable version of the first-position F chord.** Wherever you play it on the fretboard, it's always a major chord, and the 1st and 4th strings are always the root.

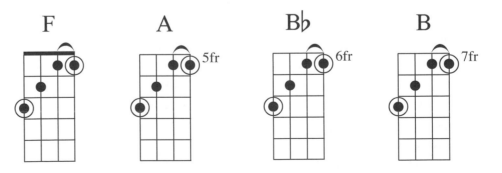

F   A   B♭   B

The three F formations of **ROADMAP #4** are G, Gm, and G7 chords.

The 1st string is the root of the F, Fm, and F7 formations. The 4th string is also the root of the F and Fm formations. If you know the notes on the 1st or 4th strings, you can play these chord formations all over the fretboard and identify them by those strings.

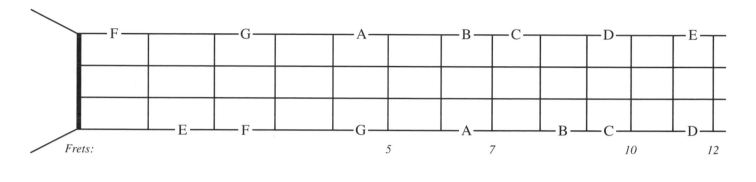

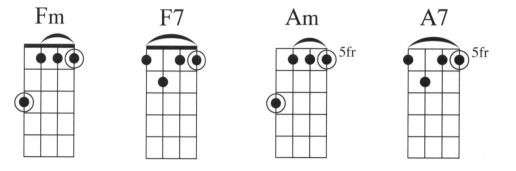

Play the three F formations all over the fretboard and name them.

F♯

F♯m

F♯7

A

Am

A7

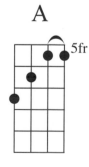

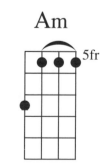

B

Bm

B7

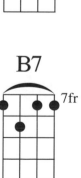

19

Compare every new chord you learn to a basic chord you already know. Every small chord grid below is a variation of the F, Fm, or F7 formation.

Here are the most-played chords. Play them and compare each formation to the larger grid to the left—the chord from which it is derived. For consistency's sake, they are all G chords.

F Major Formation (G Chord)

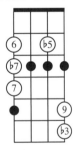

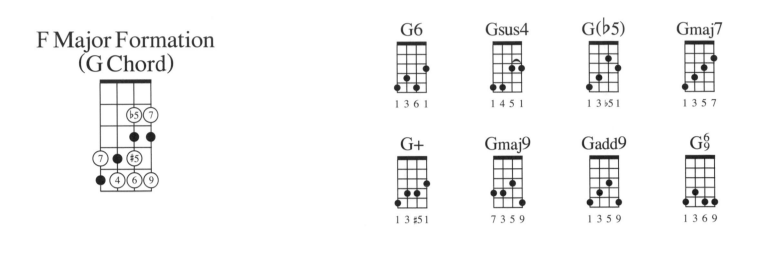

F Minor Formation (Gm Chord)

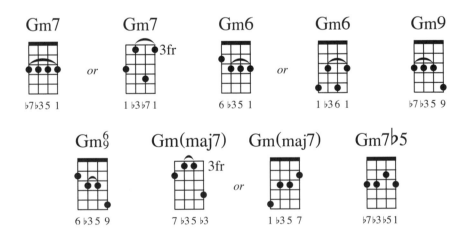

F7 Formation (G7 Chord)

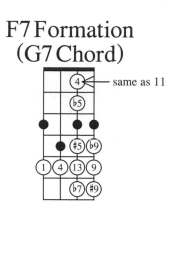

same as 11

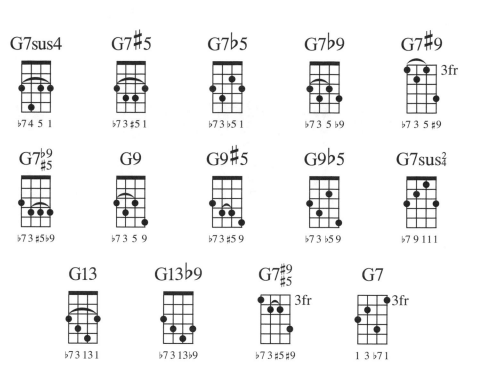

G7sus4	G7♯5	G7♭5	G7♭9	G7♯9
♭7 4 5 1	♭7 3 ♯5 1	♭7 3 ♭5 1	♭7 3 5 ♭9	♭7 3 5 ♯9 3fr

G7♭9♯5	G9	G9♯5	G9♭5	G7sus²₄
♭7 3 ♯5 ♭9	♭7 3 5 9	♭7 3 ♯5 9	♭7 3 ♭5 9	♭7 9 11 1

G13	G13♭9	G7♯9♯5	G7
♭7 3 13 1	♭7 3 13 ♭9	♭7 3 ♯5 ♯9 3fr	1 3 ♭7 1 3fr

SUMMING UP—NOW YOU KNOW...

1. Three moveable F chord formations (major, minor, and seventh) and how to play them all over the fretboard.

2. How to vary the moveable major, minor, and seventh chords to play dozens of chord types: minor sevenths, sixths, major sevenths, etc.

THE MOVEABLE B FORMATION AND ITS VARIATIONS

B Chords:

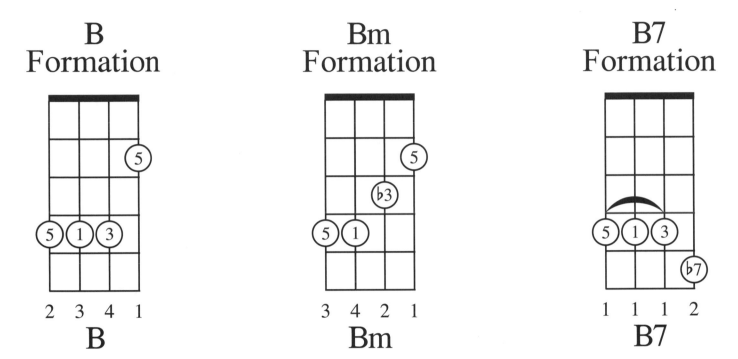

B
Formation

Bm
Formation

B7
Formation

2 3 4 1
B

3 4 2 1
Bm

1 1 1 2
B7

WHY? The three B formations of **ROADMAP #5** will help you learn another whole set of moveable chords.

WHAT? **The B formation gets its name because it's a B chord when played at the 2nd fret.** Wherever you play it on the fretboard, it's always a major chord, and the 3rd string is always the root.

B♭

C

D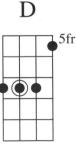

There are alternate ways to play the B and B7 formations:

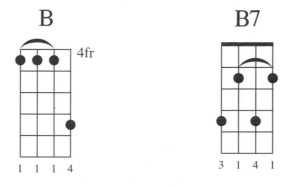

HOW? **The 3rd string is the root of the three B formations.** If you know the notes on that string, you can play these chord forms all over the fretboard and identify them:

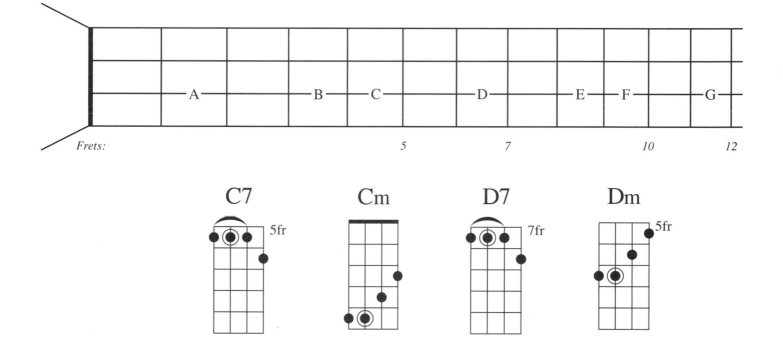

DO IT! **Play B, Bm, and B7 formations all over the fretboard and name the chords as you play them.**

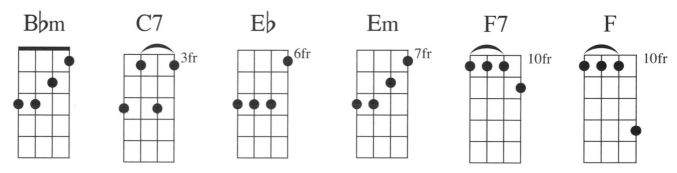

Compare every new chord you learn to a basic chord you already know. Every small chord grid that follows is a variation of a basic chord formation.

Here are the most-played chords. Play them and compare each formation to the larger grid to the left—the chord from which it is derived.

B Major Formation (B Chord)

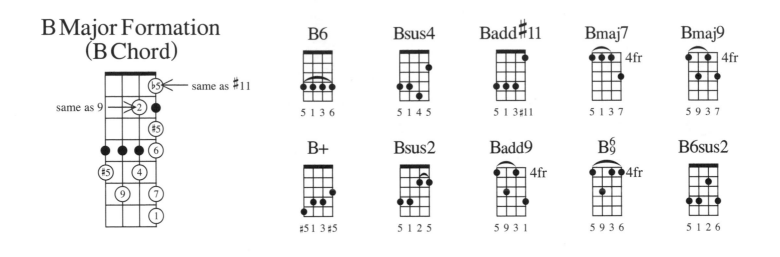

B6	Bsus4	Badd#11	Bmaj7	Bmaj9
5 1 3 6	5 1 4 5	5 1 3 #11	5 1 3 7 4fr	5 9 3 7 4fr

B+	Bsus2	Badd9	B⁶₉	B6sus2
#5 1 3 #5	5 1 2 5	5 9 3 1 4fr	5 9 3 6 4fr	5 1 2 6

B Minor Formation (Bm Chord)

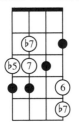

Bm7		Bm7	Bm6	Bm(maj7)	Bm7♭5
5 ♭7 ♭3 5	*or*	5 1 ♭3 ♭7	5 1 ♭3 6	5 7 ♭3 5	♭5 1 ♭3 ♭7

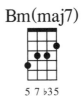

B7 Formation
(B7 Chord)

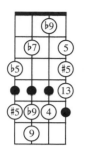

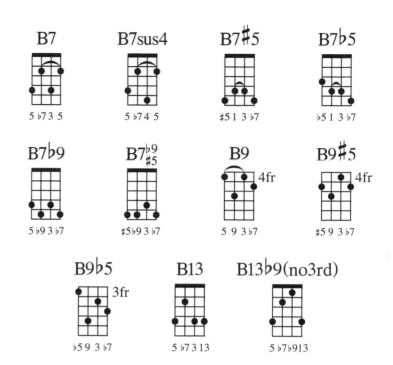

B7	B7sus4	B7#5	B7♭5
5 ♭7 3 5	5 ♭7 4 5	#5 1 3 ♭7	♭5 1 3 ♭7

B7♭9	B7♭9#5	B9	B9#5
5 ♭9 3 ♭7	#5♭9 3 ♭7	5 9 3 ♭7 (4fr)	#5 9 3 ♭7 (4fr)

B9♭5	B13	B13♭9(no3rd)
♭5 9 3 ♭7 (3fr)	5 ♭7 3 13	5 ♭7♭913

SUMMING UP—NOW YOU KNOW...

1. Five moveable B chord formations (two major, one minor, and two sevenths) and how to play them all over the fretboard.

2. How to vary these moveable formations to play dozens of chord types: minor sevenths, sixths, major sevenths, etc.

THE F–D–B ROADMAP

F Chords:

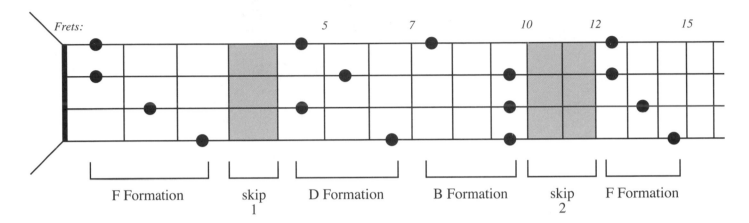

 WHY? The **F–D–B ROADMAP** shows you how to play any major chord all over the fretboard by using the three major chord formations of **ROADMAPS #3**, **4**, and **5**. It's useful for locating chords up and down the neck and for finding a higher voicing of a chord.

WHAT? The chords in the fretboard diagram above are all F chords. Play them and see!

HOW? **To memorize this roadmap, remember: F–SKIP 1, D, B–SKIP 2.** In other words, to play F chords up and down the bari fretboard:

- Play an F formation at the 1st fret (that's an F chord)…
- Then skip a fret (the 4th fret) and play a D formation, starting at the 5th fret; that's the next F chord…
- Then play a B formation at the next (8th) fret; that's the next F chord…
- Then skip two frets (the 11th and 12th) and play an F formation again, this time at the 13th fret; that's another, higher F chord.

OK, you probably can't play that last F chord; it's nearly off the fretboard of most baris. But it makes a major point about this roadmap:

*The **F–D–B ROADMAP** is an endless loop; it keeps repeating until you run out of frets.*

You can start the F–D–B loop with any chord formation. It can start with the D formation and become the D–B–F loop. The fret spacing is the same no matter where you start. For example, here are all the D chords, starting with the D formation at the 2nd fret:

D Chords:

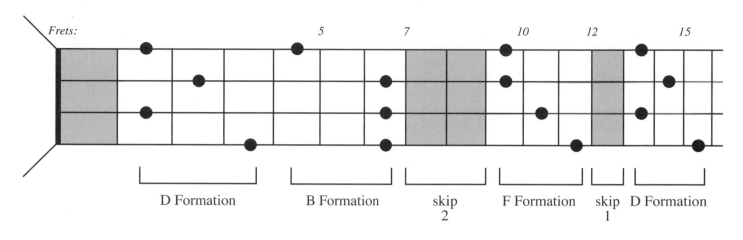

You can also start with the B formation. Here are all the C chords, starting with the B formation at the 3rd fret:

C Chords:

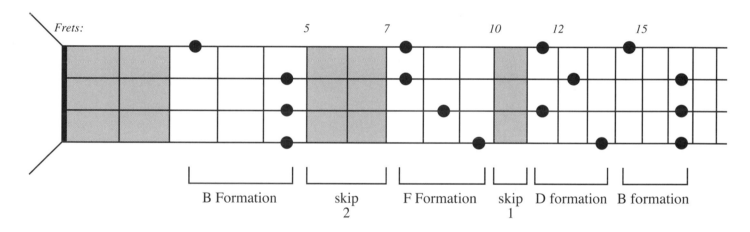

Here's the F–D–B ROADMAP with seventh chords. It includes both D7 formations, so it has four shapes instead of three:

C7 Chords:

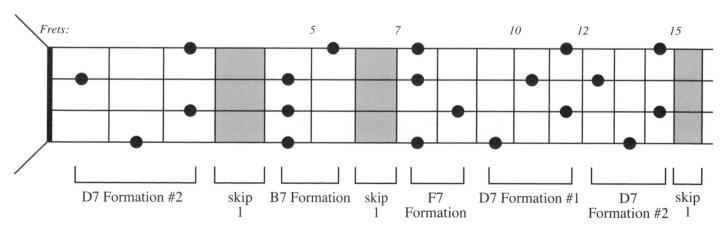

Here's the **F–D–B ROADMAP** with minor chords:

Dm Chords:

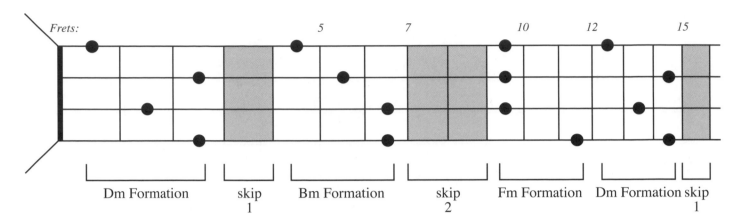

DO IT! **Practice the F–D–B ROADMAPS (major, minor, and seventh) by playing all the voicings of any one chord, going up and down the neck.** For example, strum a steady 4/4 rhythm and play all the F chords (one bar for each voicing), then all the F minor and F7 chords:

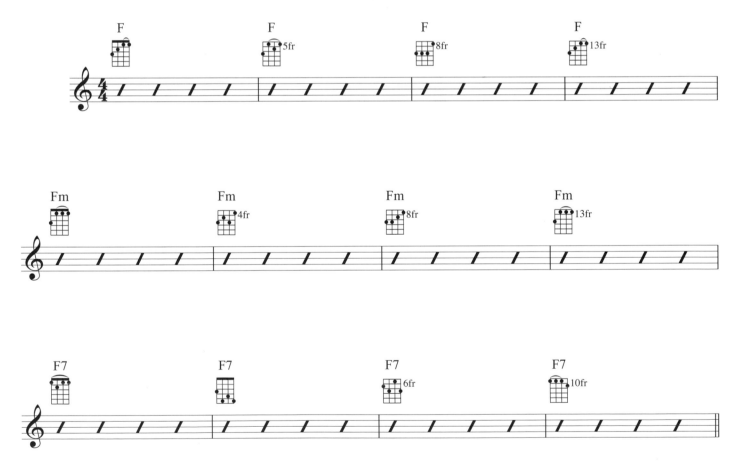

Play the following backup to the old folk song "Sloop John B." The tune lingers for several bars on each chord, giving you the opportunity to play several formations for every chord. This arrangement makes use of the first fingerpicking pattern heard on Track #6, from the Preliminaries section.

SLOOP JOHN B.—Backup

Use the F–D–B chords to play a solo to the country standard "Wabash Cannonball" in the key of G. By playing different voicings of each chord, you approximate the song's melody.

WABASH CANNONBALL

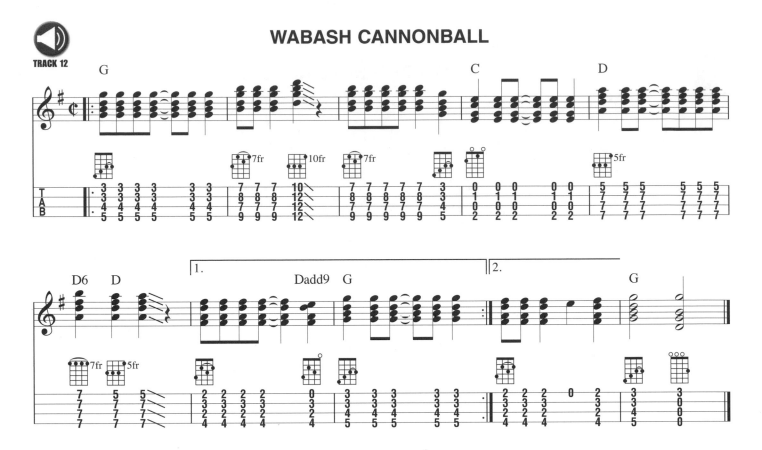

Use the minor F–D–B ROADMAP when playing backup chords to the Russian folk tune **"Meadowlands"** in the key of Am. Like "Wabash Cannonball," this arrangement almost captures the melody of the song.

MEADOWLANDS

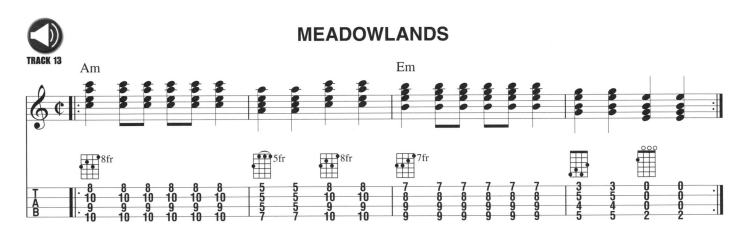

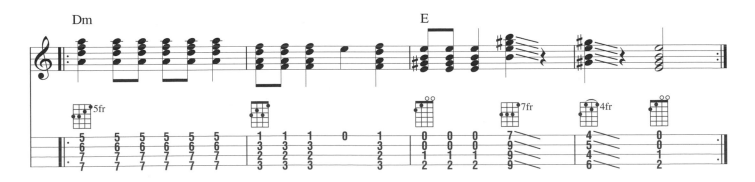

Use the seventh chord F–D–B ROADMAP to play backup for the blues tune "Betty and Dupree" in the key of C. In blues songs, it's not unusual for all the chords to be sevenths.

BETTY AND DUPREE

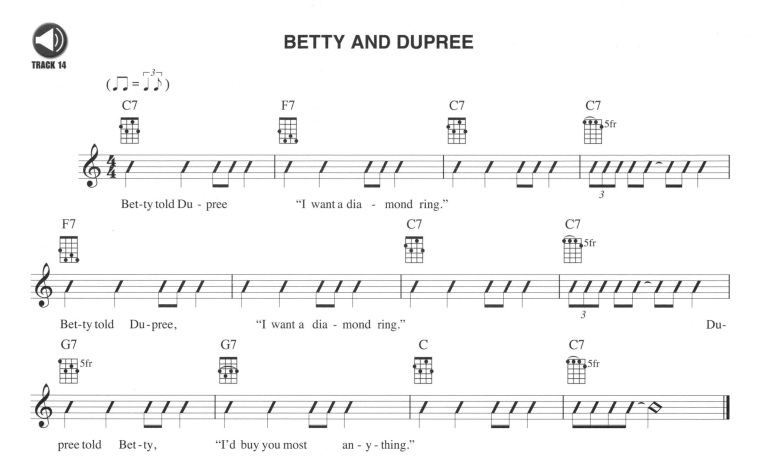

Bet-ty told Du - pree "I want a dia - mond ring."

Bet-ty told Du-pree, "I want a dia - mond ring." Du-

pree told Bet-ty, "I'd buy you most an - y - thing."

The F, D, and B formations are moveable versions of first-position chords:

- **Move the first-position E chord up a fret and it's the F formation:**

- **Move the first-position C chord up two frets and it's the D formation:**

- **Move the first-position A chord up two frets and it's the B formation:**

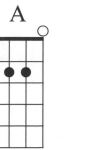

31

• Other moveable chords stem from first-position chords:

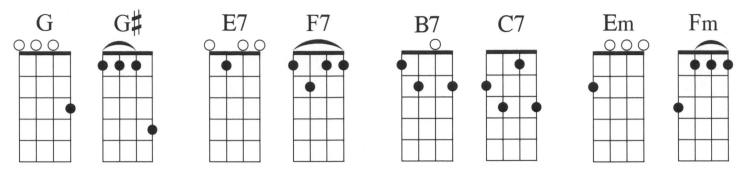

Apply these concepts to the F—D—B ROADMAP and you can find all the higher voicings of first-position chords:

C Chords:

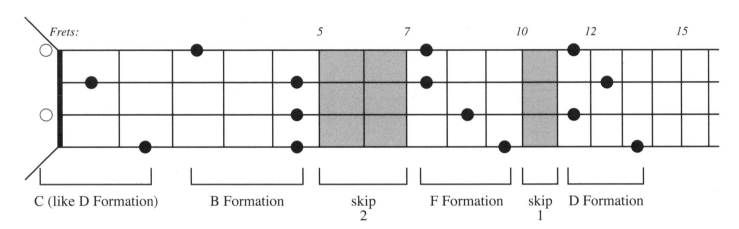

| C (like D Formation) | B Formation | skip 2 | F Formation | skip 1 | D Formation |

E Chords:

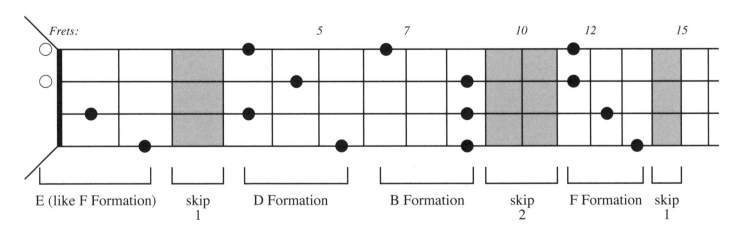

| E (like F Formation) | skip 1 | D Formation | B Formation | skip 2 | F Formation | skip 1 |

SUMMING UP—NOW YOU KNOW...

1. How to use F, D, and B formations to play any major chord all over the fretboard.

2. How to use Fm, Dm, and Bm formations to play any minor chord all over the fretboard.

3. How to use F7, D7, and B7 formations to play any seventh chord all over the fretboard.

CHORD FAMILIES

Three G Chord Families:

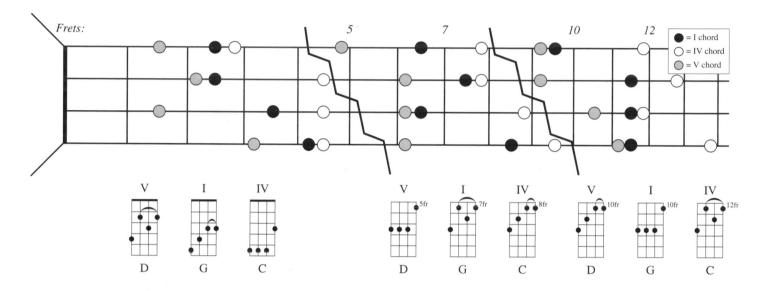

V   I   IV   V   I   IV   V   I   IV

D   G   C   D   G   C   D   G   C

WHY?
It's easier to learn new tunes and create solos or play backup when you understand chord families and know how to play them all over the fretboard. **ROADMAP #7** arranges the three moveable major chords (F, D, and B formations) into chord families. It helps you hear common chord changes and play them automatically.

WHAT?
Every song has a chord progression—a repeated chord sequence in which each chord is played for a certain number of bars.

Thousands of tunes consist of just three chords: the I, IV, and V. These three chords are a "chord family." "I," "IV," and "V" refer to steps of the major scale of your key.

- The I chord is the key center. In the key of C, C is the I chord because C is the first note in the C major scale.

- The IV chord is the chord whose root is the fourth note in the major scale of your key. In the key of C, F is the IV chord since F is the fourth note in the C major scale.

- The V chord is the chord whose root is the fifth note in the major scale of your key. In the key of C, G is the V chord since G is the fifth note in the C major scale.

ROADMAP #7 shows three ways of playing the "key of G" chord family: with an F-formation I chord, with a B-formation I chord, and with a D-formation I chord.

The relationships in ROADMAP #7 are moveable. Once you learn them, you can make chord changes automatically.
For example, in any key, if you're playing a *I chord* with an F formation, the *V chord* is a D formation one fret lower.

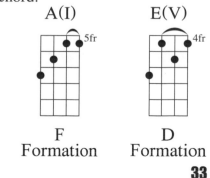

A(I)   E(V)

F   D
Formation Formation

HOW? Practice playing different chord families, combining **ROADMAPS #7** and **#6** (the **F–D–B ROADMAP**). For example, here are three key-of-D chord families:

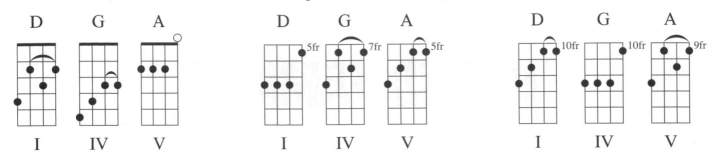

D	G	A	D	G	A	D	G	A
I	IV	V	I	IV	V	I	IV	V

Strum the following progression in many keys, all over the fretboard. It fits a number of well-known tunes, including "Louie Louie," "La Bamba," "Wild Thing," "Twist and Shout," and "Good Lovin'," so hum one of those tunes while you strum! It'll help you get so familiar with the I–IV–V chord relationships that they'll become automatic—especially if you do this all over the fretboard in different keys and keep a steady rhythm while you're strumming.

TRACK 15

For example, in the key of G:

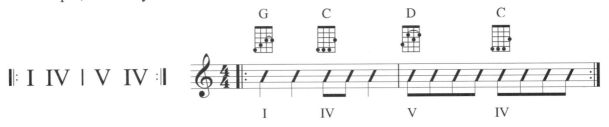

‖: I IV | V IV :‖

Learn to recognize the sound of a V chord and a IV chord. Here's a good exercise to help you do this:

- Strum any chord four times (C, for example).
- Keeping a steady rhythm, strum its V chord (G) four times.
- Do this with many different chords, all over the fretboard, until you recognize the "sound" of going from I to V.
- Repeat the same process all over the fretboard, this time going from I to IV.

DO IT! Play "Midnight Special" to practice memorizing the chord-family relationships. While you're strumming it, be aware that you're playing this progression: I–IV–I–V–I.

TRACK 16

THE MIDNIGHT SPECIAL

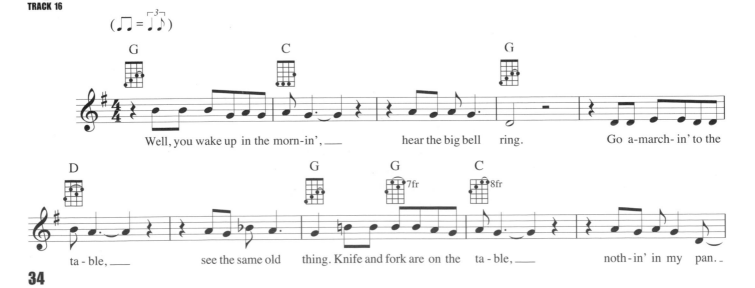

Well, you wake up in the morn-in', ___ hear the big bell ring. Go a-march-in' to the ta-ble, ___ see the same old thing. Knife and fork are on the ta-ble, ___ noth-in' in my pan. _

34

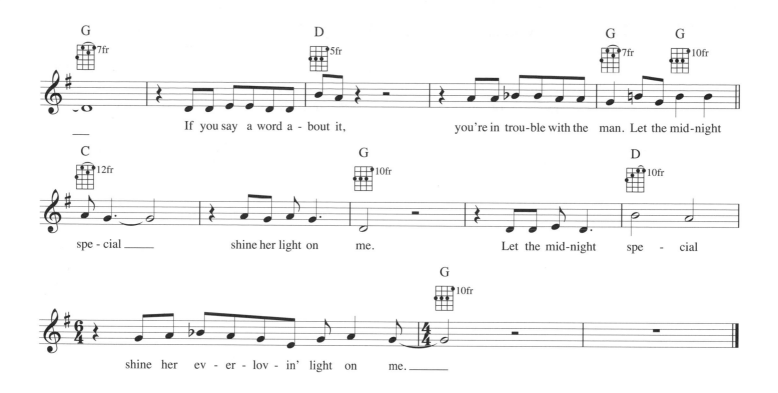

Play the following cowboy song, "Streets of Laredo," in Eb. As you play it, be aware of which chords are I (Eb), IV (Ab), and V (Bb). Then try playing it in other keys.

STREETS OF LAREDO

I, IV, and V are the only chords you need to play a 12-bar blues. This famous chord progression is the basis of countless blues, rock, country, bluegrass, and swing tunes. Some famous songs with the 12-bar blues format include "Stormy Monday," "Route 66," "Hound Dog," "Whole Lotta Shakin' Goin' on," "Shake, Rattle and Roll," "Johnny B. Goode," and "Kansas City." There are a lot of variations of the 12-bar blues, but here's the basic pattern in G:

$$\frac{4}{4}\| \text{G} | ⁄ | ⁄ | ⁄ | \text{C} | ⁄ | \text{G} | ⁄ | \text{D} | ⁄ | \text{G} | ⁄ \|$$
$$\quad\; \text{I} \qquad\qquad\qquad\quad \text{IV} \qquad \text{I} \qquad\quad \text{V} \qquad \text{I}$$

Each of the 12 bars (measures) in the above blues progression has four beats. The repeat sign (⁄) means "repeat the previous bar."

"Hesitation Blues," below, goes back nearly a century. After playing it, strum it again and hum any of the other blues tunes mentioned above.

TRACK 18

HESITATION BLUES

36

The V chord is always two frets above the IV chord and vice versa (the IV chord is always two frets below the V chord). That means you have alternative ways to play your I–IV–V chord families:

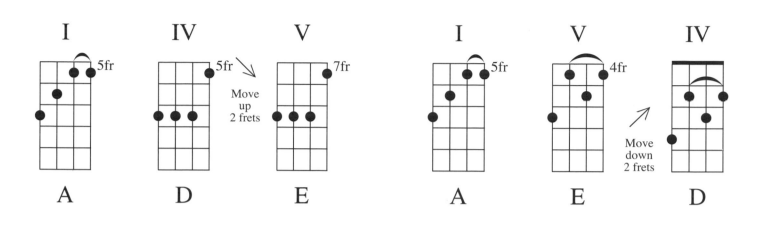

I	IV	V		I	V	IV
A	D	E		A	E	D

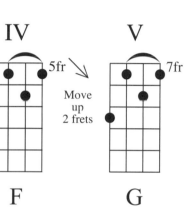 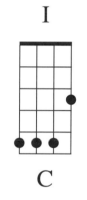 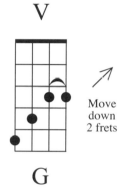 

I	IV	V		I	V	IV
C	F	G		C	G	F

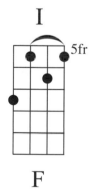 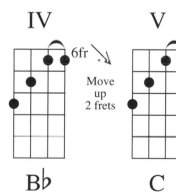 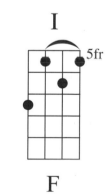 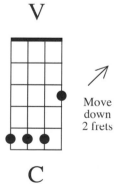 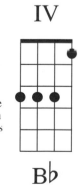

I	IV	V		I	V	IV
F	B♭	C		F	C	B♭

The gospel tune "Oh Mary, Don't You Weep" makes use of these alternate IV and V chords:

OH MARY, DON'T YOU WEEP

You can remap the I–IV–V chord families with seventh and ninth chords. This enables you to enhance your blues backup since blues tunes are often composed of seventh or ninth chords instead of major chords.

Here are the C chord families converted to seventh and ninth chords, followed by a bluesier version of "Hesitation Blues":

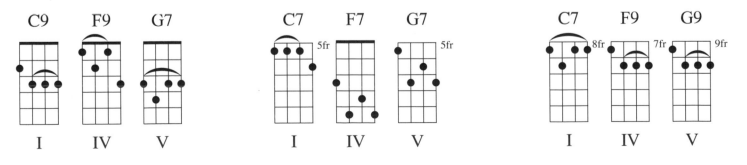

HESITATION BLUES—with Seventh and Ninth Chords

Ea-gle on a dol-lar says, "In God We Trust." _ Wom-an says she wants a man but wants to see a dol-lar first. Tell me

how long _ must I wait? _ Can I get you now, _

or must I hes-i - tate? _ Got the hes-i-tat-in' feet, hes-i-tat-in' shoes,

an-gels up in heav-en sing the hes-i-ta-tion blues. Tell me how long _ must I wait? _

Can I get you now, _ or must I hes-i - tate? _

SUMMING UP—NOW YOU KNOW...

1. How to locate three different chord families for any key using major or seventh chords.

2. How to use all three chord families to play tunes using major or seventh chords.

3. An alternate way to locate IV and V chords.

4. The meaning of these musical terms:

   a) I Chord   d) Chord Family

   b) IV Chord   e) 12-Bar Blues

   c) V Chord

CHORD SOLOING

Major
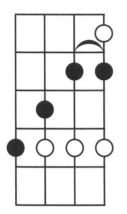

Major
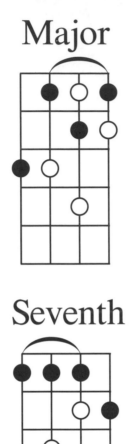

Major
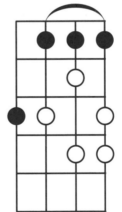

Seventh
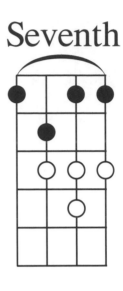

Ninth
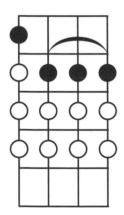

Seventh

Minor

Minor
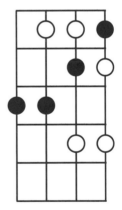

WHY? Bari players can do more than strum an accompaniment; they can play songs, just like a pianist or guitarist, in the form of *chord solos*—chords and melody played at the same time. Learn how to vary your moveable chords à la **ROADMAP #8** and you'll be able to play instrumental solos on the baritone in addition to (or instead of) strumming backup.

WHAT? **To play chord-melody solos, strum the chord voicing whose top (highest) note is the melody note.** The idea is to put the melody on the 1st or 2nd string, where it stands out, and to harmonize it with the other notes in the chord.

You don't need a chord for every melody note. It's sufficient to play a chord with the first note of a melodic phrase.

Play a chord with every chord change that occurs, whether it's at the beginning or in the middle of a melodic phrase. By this standard, you wind up playing one or two chords per bar of music.

Each chord shape in ROADMAP #8 is surrounded by circled (white) notes that can be played with the basic chord formation. If the melody note is not in the basic chord shape, it's probably one of these "extra" notes. Sometimes you can add a "circled note" with a spare fretting finger; sometimes you change fingering to flat a note.

You've seen the chord grids of **ROADMAP #8** in Chapters 3, 4, and 5. You can use any of the major, minor, and seventh chords in those chapters to play chord solos; these are some of the most useful shapes.

You can also follow a song's chord progression and ad-lib solos by playing chord-based licks.

HOW?

Play the following chord-based licks. Keep your left hand loosely in the pictured chord position. These samples show how you can play chords and melody at the same time.

TRACK 21

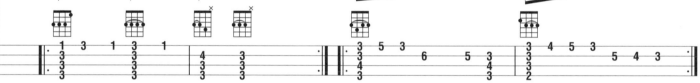

First-position chords (chords that include open strings) can also be used in chord solos. The "extra notes" of **ROADMAP #8** can be applied to first-position chords if you relate each one to its equivalent moveable chord. Lower each of the following moveable chords one fret and you get a familiar first-position chord:

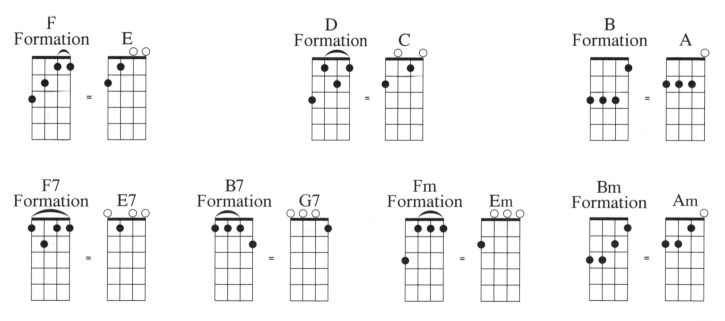

Here are some chord-melody solos for familiar tunes. As you play them, notice how *you sometimes have to play a higher or lower voicing of a chord* in order to reach a higher or lower melody note.

LITTLE BROWN JUG

The following solo shows how to ad-lib with chord-based licks. It's an improvisation based on "Little Brown Jug." Jazz players usually state the melody of a tune (as in the previous arrangement of "Little Brown Jug") and then make up solos based on the song's chord progression, like this:

LITTLE BROWN JUG—Ad-Lib

TRACK 23

Play this chord solo for "Aura Lee," the old folk song that was the basis for Elvis Presley's "Love Me Tender."

AURA LEE

TRACK 24

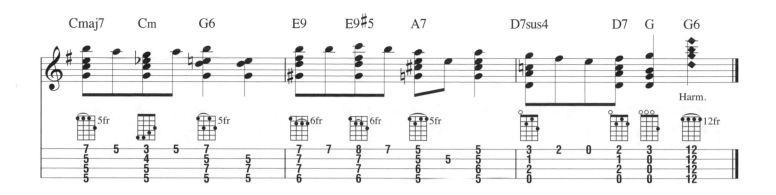

Here's a chord-melody arrangement of "Hesitation Blues," which you played in the previous chapter.

HESITATION BLUES—Chord Melody

TRACK 25

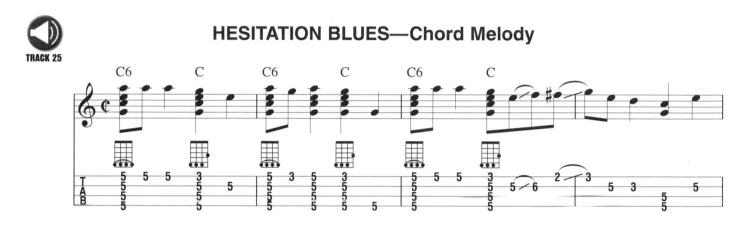

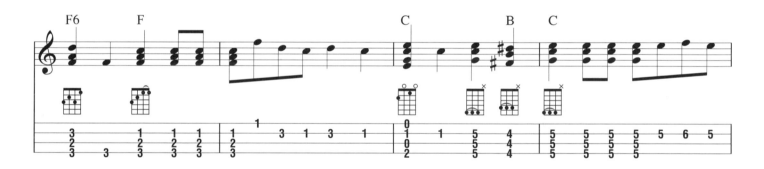

SUMMING UP—NOW YOU KNOW...

1. How to base licks and solos on moveable chord formations.
2. How to play a chord-melody solo using moveable chords and chord-based licks.
3. How to improvise, chord-style, over a chord progression.

FIRST-POSITION MAJOR SCALES

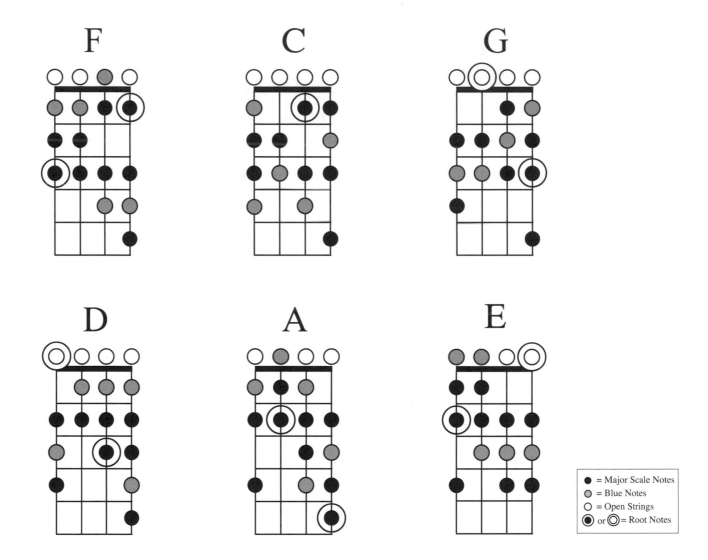

WHY? It's easier to play a song's melody or improvise a solo when you're familiar with major scales.

WHAT? **Every key has its own scale and characteristic licks.** You use the C major scale to play in the key of C, the E major scale to play in E, and so on.

Often, a scale (and the licks that go with it) can be played throughout a tune, in spite of chord changes within the tune.

The *root* is the note that gives the scale its name.

The root notes are circled in the ROADMAP #9 diagrams above.

The gray circles are "blue notes"—flatted 3rds, 5ths, and 7ths. They add a bluesy flavor to the scales.

HOW? Put your hand "in position" for each scale by fingering the appropriate chord (e.g., play an A chord to get in position for the A major scale). You don't have to maintain the chord while playing the scale; it's just a reference point.

Play up and down each scale until it feels comfortable and familiar. Play the chord before playing the scale and then loop the scale—play it several times in a row, with no pause between repetitions. Here are the six easiest scales to practice:

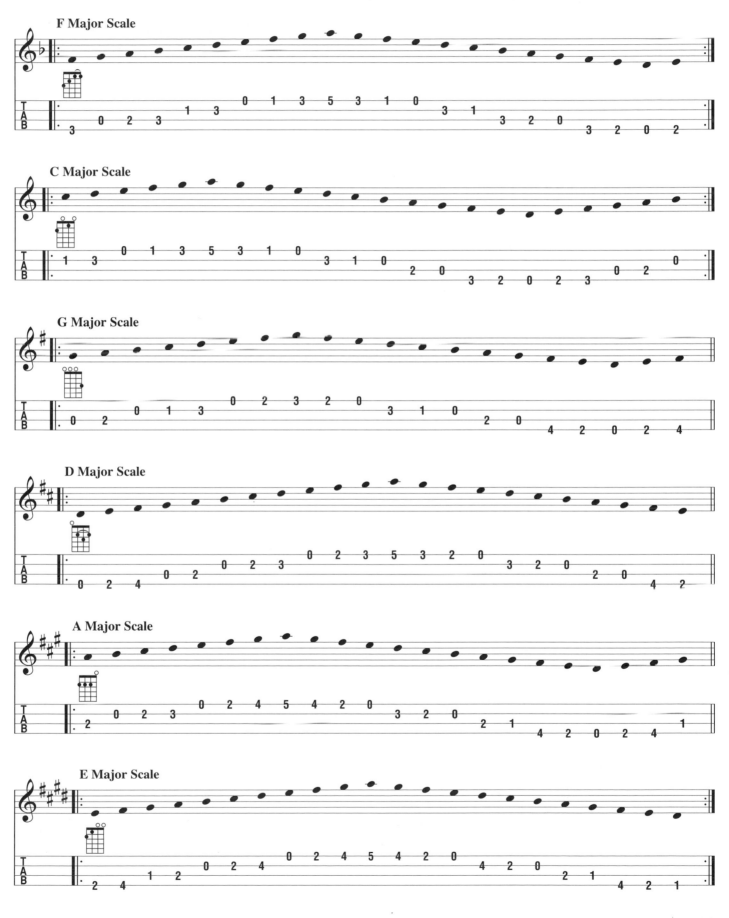

DO IT! **Try playing familiar melodies in several keys:**

- Play any major scale (C, for example).
- Strum a C chord to establish the key and, just using your ear, try to play the melody to "Twinkle Twinkle, Little Star." How hard could it be?
- Do the same thing in a different key.
- Do the same thing with a different tune.

Often, you can play tunes and ad-lib melodies by using the major scale that matches your key, especially if you add occasional blue notes—there's no need to change scales with every chord in the song! If you're playing a song in the key of C, you can probably play the melody by using the C major scale. If you're jamming with another player who's playing chords (on another uke, bari, guitar, or any chording instrument), you can improvise single-note solos by using that same C major scale.

The following single-note solos show how to use all six major scales to play a tune and ornament it with colorful licks. These improvisations are based on "Aloha 'Oe," the famous Hawaiian farewell song. Each solo shows how to embellish the song's melody by using major scales and adding occasional blue notes.

Listen to Track 26 to learn the basic melody of "Aloha 'Oe."

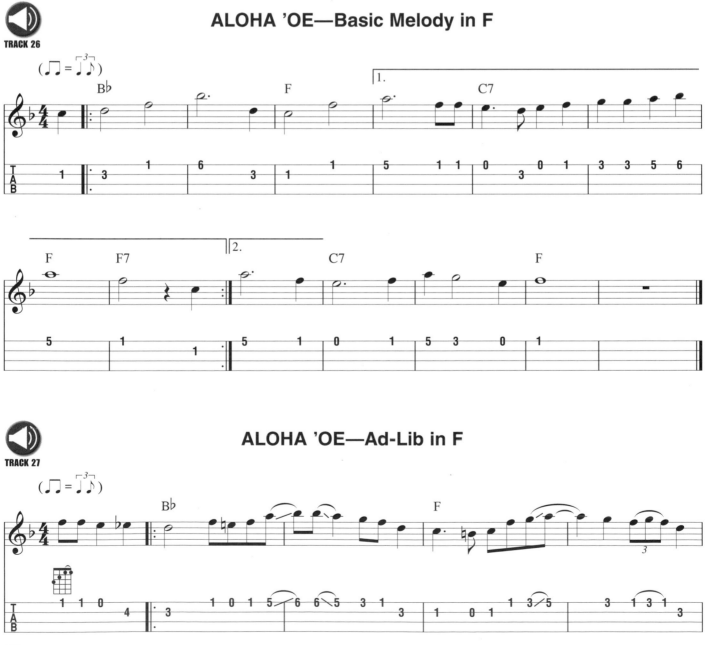

ALOHA 'OE—Basic Melody in F

TRACK 26

ALOHA 'OE—Ad-Lib in F

TRACK 27

ALOHA 'OE—Ad-Lib in C

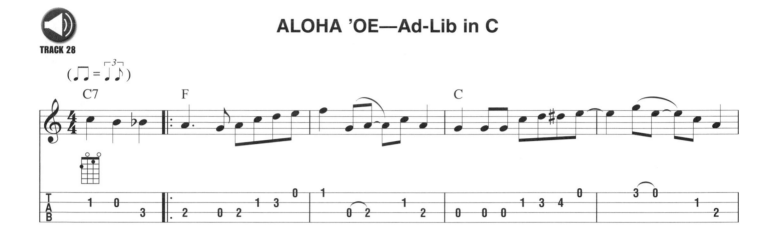

ALOHA 'OE—Ad-Lib in G

ALOHA 'OE—Ad-Lib in D

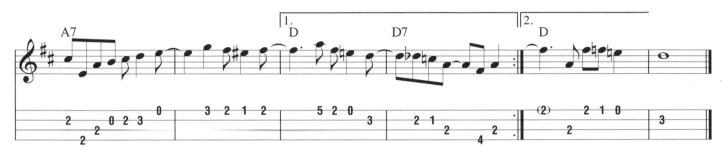

ALOHA 'OE—Ad-Lib in A

TRACK 32

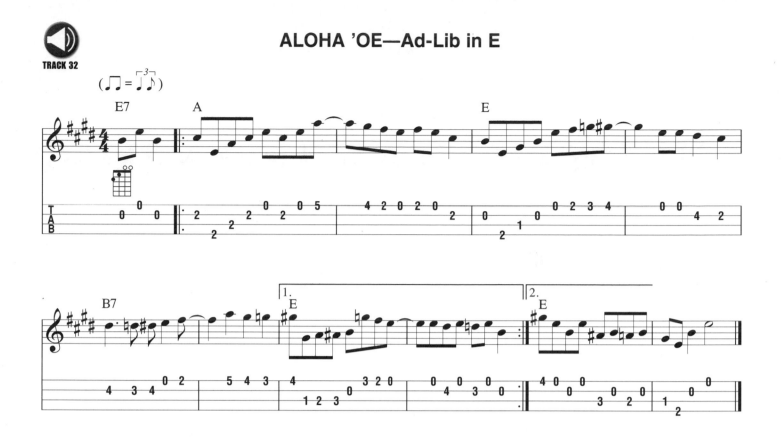

Do the same thing with other familiar tunes like "This Land Is Your Land" or "Yellow Submarine." Play the song's melody in different keys, then try to embellish the melody with slides and extra notes.

SUMMING UP—NOW YOU KNOW...

1. How to play six first-position major scales (F, C, G, D, A, and E) and how to use them to play licks and solos.

2. The meaning of the musical term "blue notes" and how to add them to your major scales and licks.

FOUR MOVEABLE MAJOR SCALES

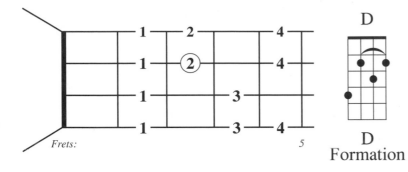

D
D
Formation

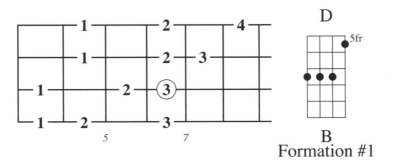

D
B
Formation #1

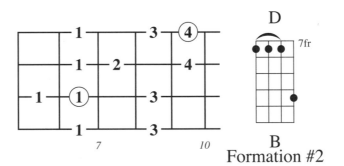

D
B
Formation #2

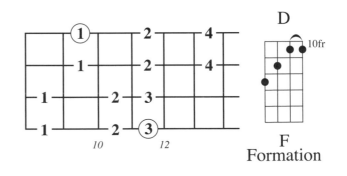

D
F
Formation

WHY? The moveable major scales help you play melodies and ad-lib solos in any key, all over the fretboard. They bring you a step closer to any player's goal: to be able to play whatever you can hear.

WHAT? The numbers on the fretboard in **ROADMAP #10** are left-hand fingering suggestions.

The four scales of **ROADMAP #10** are based on the moveable chord shapes of **ROADMAPS #3, 4, and 5** (the D, F, and B shapes). The root notes (Ds) are circled. Play the appropriate chord shape to get your fretting hand in position to play its corresponding major scale. For example, play the F formation at the 10th fret to play the highest D scale of **ROADMAP #10**.

Like the first-position major scales of **ROADMAP #9**, one moveable major scale can often be used to play a whole tune—that is, both the melody *and* improvisation. You don't have to change scales with each chord change. If a song is in the key of G, use the G major scale throughout.

HOW? Here are the four D major scales that match the D, F, and B formations (there are two scales that match the B formation). Play each chord shape before playing the scale. Start each scale with its root note so you can recognize the "do-re-mi" sound you have heard all your life!

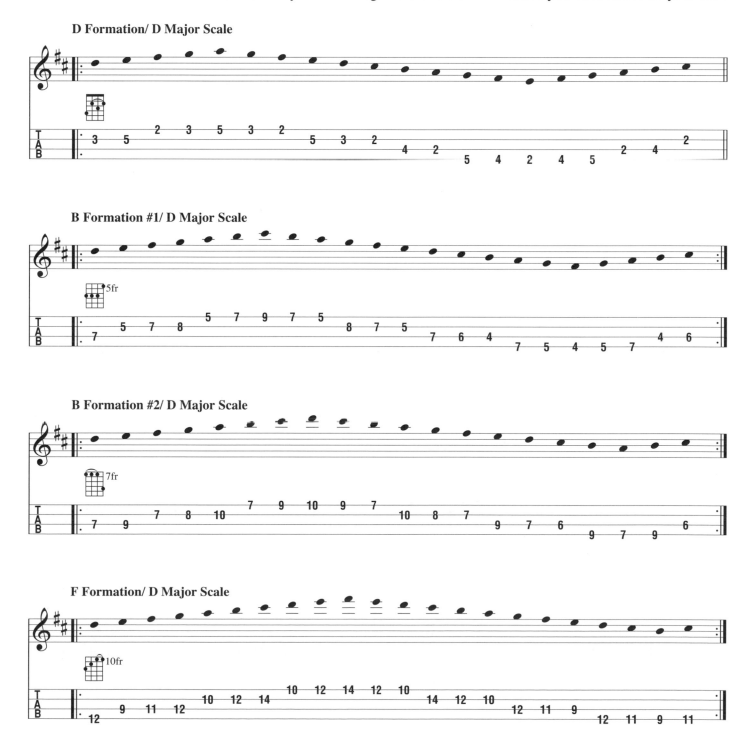

You can move the moveable major scales around, using their root notes to locate any scale you want. If a song is in G, you can use these four major scales:

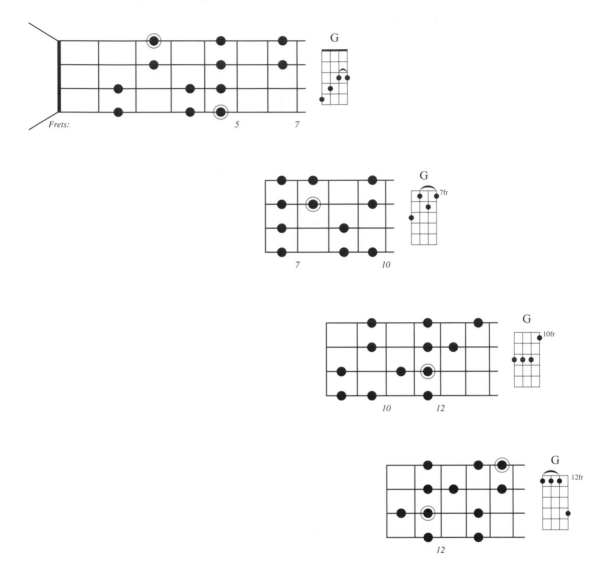

You can use the moveable major scales to play melodies and improvise solos, just as you did with the first-position scales of **ROADMAP #9.** But now you can play in any key, and you can choose whether to play in a high, low, or medium register for each key.

DO IT! Use major scales to play melodies. For example, here's the melody to "Buffalo Gals" in B♭. After playing it, try it in B by moving everything up a fret; then do it again in A, moving it down a fret from the B♭ version.

TRACK 33

BUFFALO GALS—Melody in B♭ (B Formation)

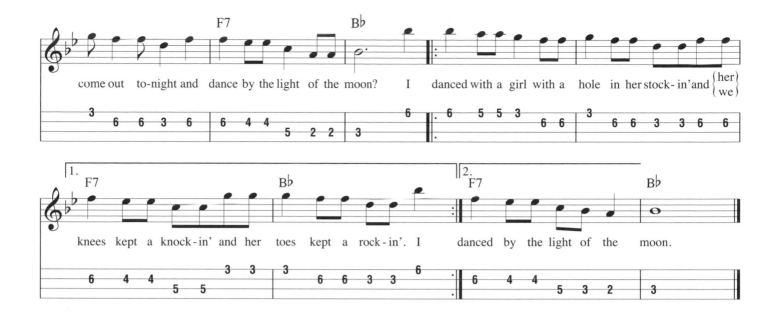

come out to-night and dance by the light of the moon? I danced with a girl with a hole in her stock-in'and {her} {we}

1.
knees kept a knock-in' and her toes kept a rock-in'. I

2.
danced by the light of the moon.

Use major scales to improvise solos. Soloists often ad-lib melodies and licks over a familiar tune. For example, after playing the melody to "Buffalo Gals," you might improvise a solo over the same chord changes, using the same B-formation major scale.

TRACK 34

BUFFALO GALS—Ad-Lib Solo in B♭ (B Formation)

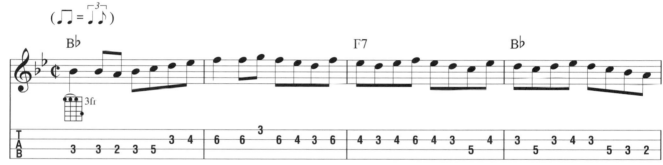

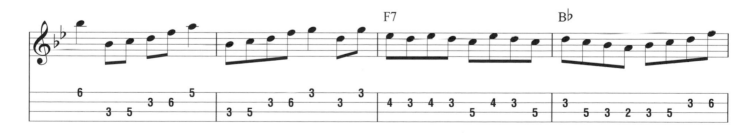

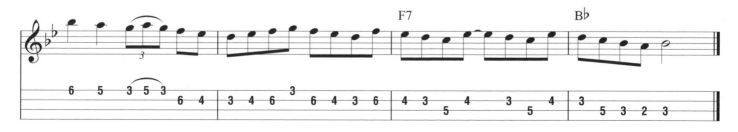

Here's "In the Good Old Summertime" in the key of F. As you did with "Buffalo Gals," play the arrangement below, then play it in different keys, using the F formation: play it in A, B♭, and so on.

IN THE GOOD OLD SUMMERTIME—Melody in F (F Formation)

"Oh, My Darling Clementine," below, makes use of the D-formation major scale. Play it as written, then move it up to E, F, G, etc.

OH, MY DARLING CLEMENTINE—Melody in D (D Formation)

TRACK 36

In addition to freely improvising, you can use major scales to ornament a given melody. Here's an ad-lib solo to "Oh, My Darling Clementine." The melody is made fancier by the inclusion of "extra notes" from the D major scale. To do this type of embellishment, surround the sustained melody notes with scale increments. For example, if the melody has a sustained G note:

- Play G–F#–E–F#–G (dipping below the melody note and coming back to it), or
- Play G–A–B–A–G (going above the melody note and coming back to it), or
- Play G–F#–G–A–G (circling around the melody note).

OH, MY DARLING CLEMENTINE—Ornamented Melodic Solo in D (D Formation)

TRACK 37

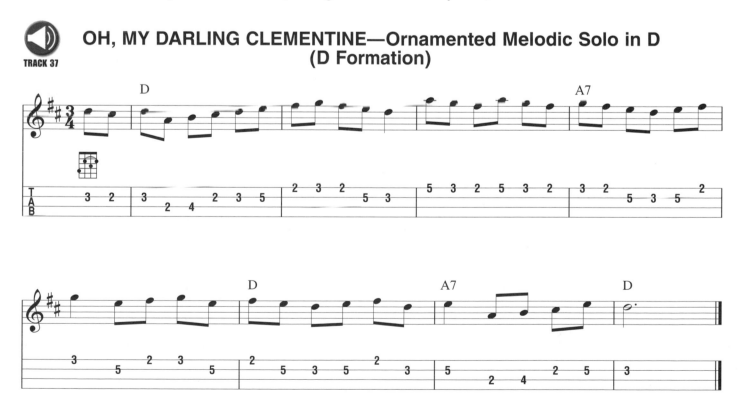

Some songs have such a wide range that it takes two scale positions to play them:

AVALON—Melody in D (D and B Formations)

Many melodies include a few "accidentals"—notes that are not in the major scale of their key. Familiarity with the major scale makes it easy to find these notes, as they're always one fret above or below the major scale notes. For example:

TRACK 39

MOONLIGHT BAY—Melody in E (D Formation)

We were sail - ing a - long on Moon - light Bay.
"You have stol - en my heart; now don't go 'way,"

We could hear the voic - es ring - ing. They seemed to say:

as we sang love's old, sweet song on Moon - light Bay.

SUMMING UP—NOW YOU KNOW...

1. How to play four moveable major scales for each key.

2. How to use them to play melodies.

3. How to use them to ornament a melody and ad-lib solos.

4. The meaning of the musical term "accidental."

THE CIRCLE OF FIFTHS

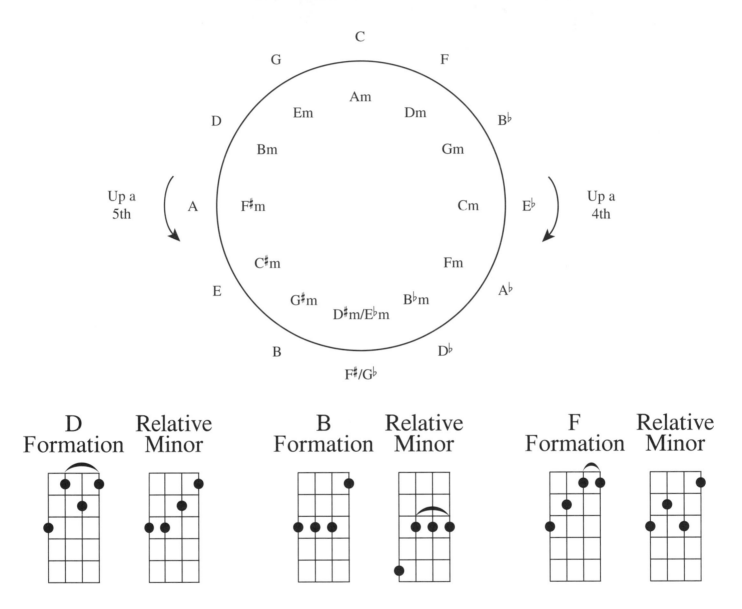

WHY? Many songs include more than just the I, IV, and V chords. These subtler chord progressions are easier to understand and play once you are acquainted with relative minors and circle-of-fifths movement.

WHAT? The circle of fifths (also called the "circle of fourths") arranges the 12 musical notes so that a **step counter-clockwise takes you up a 5th, and a step clockwise takes you up a 4th.**

- Counter-clockwise: G is a 5th above C; D is a 5th above G, etc.
- Clockwise: F is a 4th above C; B♭ is a 4th above F, etc.

Every major chord has a relative minor chord that has many of the same notes as its relative major. The relative minor is the vi chord; A is the sixth note of the C major scale, so Am is the relative minor of a C major chord. Notice the similarities between the two chords. (The use of lowercase Roman numerals, as in the vi chord, indicates *minor chords*.)

Am is the relative minor of C; C is the relative major of Am.

If a song includes minor chords, they are usually the relative minors of the I, IV, and V chords. A song in the key of C may include Am (relative minor of C), Dm (relative minor of F, the IV chord), or Em (relative minor of G, the V chord).

The chord grids in ROADMAP #11 show how to alter each of the three moveable major chords to play its relative minor:

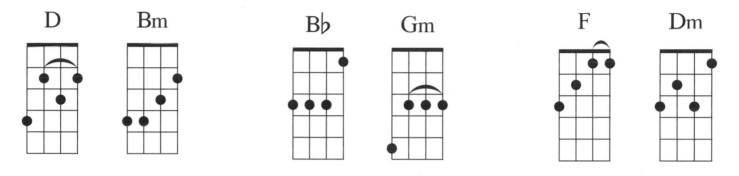

A song has "circle-of-fifths" chord movement if the chords move up by 4ths; for example, in the key of G: E7–A7–D7–G, or Em–Am–Dm–G.

HOW? In circle-of-fifths progressions, you leave the I chord, creating tension, and resolve the tension by using clockwise motion to come back to I, going up by 4ths until you are "home" (at the I chord). For example, in "Raggy Blues," which follows, you jump from C to the A7 chord (leaving the C chord family) and then get back to C by going clockwise along the circle: D7 is a 4th above A7, G7 is a 4th above D7, and C is a 4th above G7. Strum the progression using four downstrokes per bar. It resembles "Alice's Restaurant" and many other tunes, including Robert Johnson's "They're Red Hot" and Bob Wills's "Bring It on Down to My House, Honey."

RAGGY BLUES

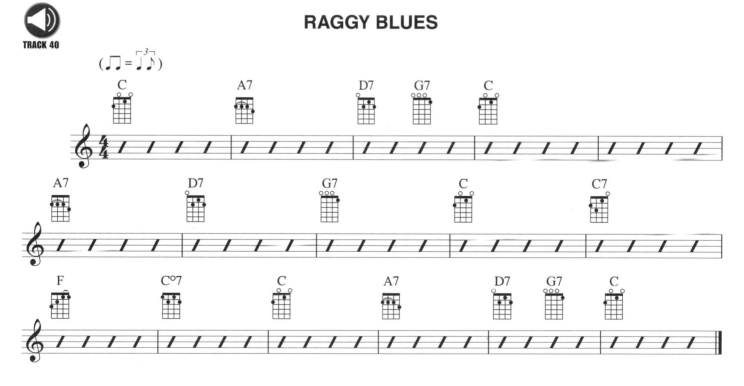

This is a I–VI–II–V progression because C is I, A is a 6th above C, D is a 2nd above C, and G is a 5th above C.

As you move clockwise along the circle, **the chords can be major or minor, but the V chord is almost always a seventh chord.**

If you use moveable chords, you can play a circle-of-fifths-type progression (moving up by 4ths) automatically. In ROADMAP #7, you learned how to go up a 4th from any of the moveable major chord formations:

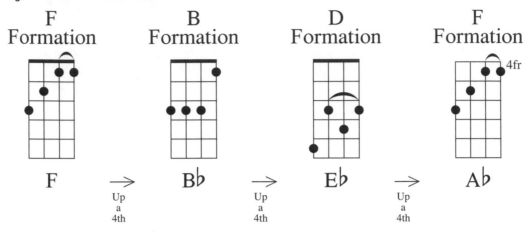

You can do the same thing with minor chords:

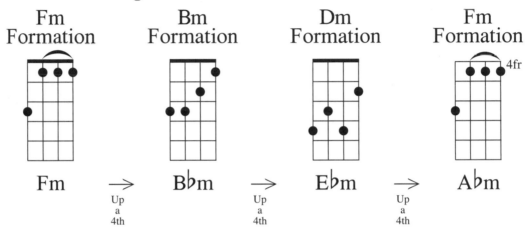

With moveable seventh chords, you have two or more ways to move up a 4th:

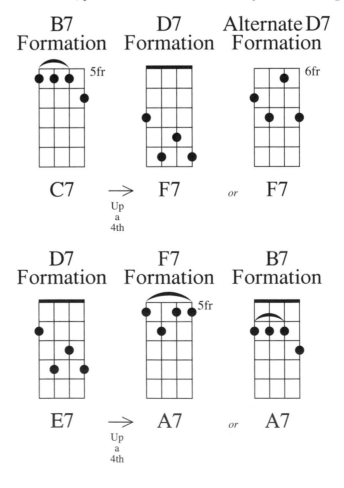

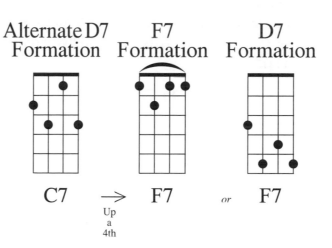

Alternate D7 Formation → C7 → F7 Up a 4th

F7 Formation → F7 or F7

D7 Formation

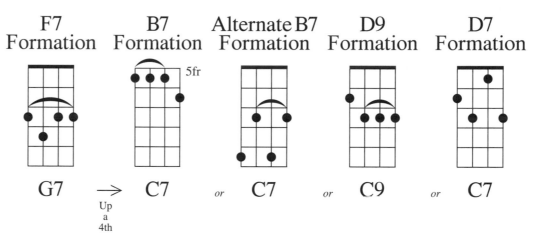

F7 Formation → G7 → C7 Up a 4th

B7 Formation → C7 or C7

Alternate B7 Formation → C9 or C7

D9 Formation

D7 Formation

Here are some ways to play a series of seventh chords that move up by 4ths:

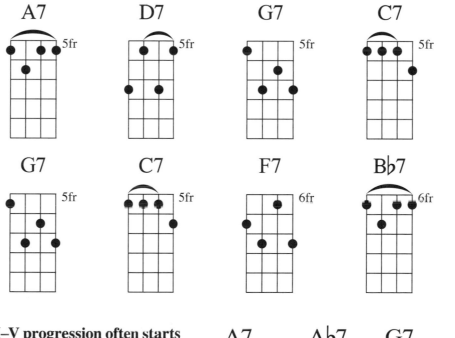

A7   D7   G7   C7

G7   C7   F7   B♭7

The I–VI–II–V progression often starts with a series of descending chords that take you from I to VI. In fact, whenever you hear chords walking down three frets *chromatically* (one fret at a time), it usually means you're going from I to VI and starting a I–VI–II–V–I progression. It's the beginning of "Sweet Georgia Brown," "(Up a) Lazy River," "I Ain't Got Nobody," and many more:

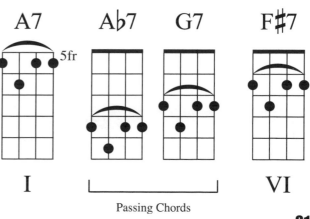

A7   A♭7   G7   F♯7

I   Passing Chords   VI

Many songs contain a III–VI–II–V–I circle-of-fifths sequence. If it's in the *bridge* (a middle section of a tune, usually eight bars long) and the chords are all sevenths, it's referred to as the "I Got Rhythm bridge." Notice how easy it is to play this progression by using two chord positions:

I GOT RHYTHM Bridge

TRACK 41

In all the circle-of-fifths chord progressions you've seen so far, seventh chords have "cycled back" to the I chord. *Often, minor chords are involved instead of (or in addition to) seventh chords.* In fact, one of the most often-used chord progressions is the I–vi–ii–V7–I progression. In the key of C, that's C–Am–Dm–G7–C. After jumping from C (the I chord) to Am (the vi chord), you move up by 4ths to get back to C.

DO IT! **Play the I–vi–ii–V7 progression in many keys.** This progression is so common that pros have nicknamed it "standard changes," the "dime store progression," "ice cream changes," and "I Got Rhythm changes" (after the Gershwin song)—or just "rhythm changes" for short. It's the basis for countless standards (e.g., "Blue Moon," "Heart and Soul," and "These Foolish Things") and classic rock tunes ("Oh, Donna," "You Send Me," "Stand by Me," "Everytime You Go Away," and "Every Breath You Take"). Try humming one of these songs while strumming this progression:

I–vi–ii–V7 PROGRESSION

TRACK 42

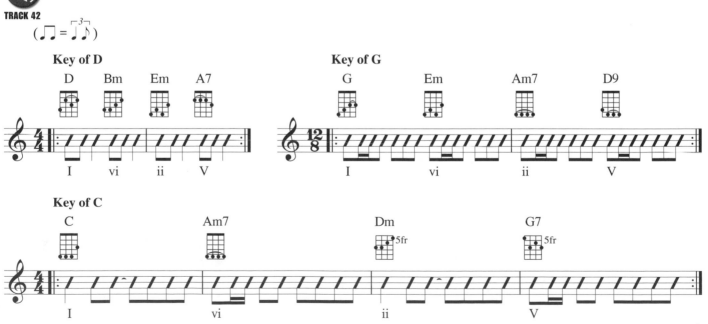

Sometimes the IV chord is played instead of the minor ii chord. It's a small change because the IV chord is the relative major of ii. In the key of C, for example, Dm is ii, and F, its relative major, is IV.

Play I–VII–III–VI–II–V–I progressions, like "Mister Sandman" and "Red Roses for a Blue Lady." In these tunes, you jump halfway around the circle, from I (or C, in the key of C) to VII (B7), then you use circle-of-fifths movement to get back to C, going up a 4th (from B7 to E7), up another 4th (to A7), and so on until you reach the C chord:

I–VII–III–VI–II–V–I PROGRESSION

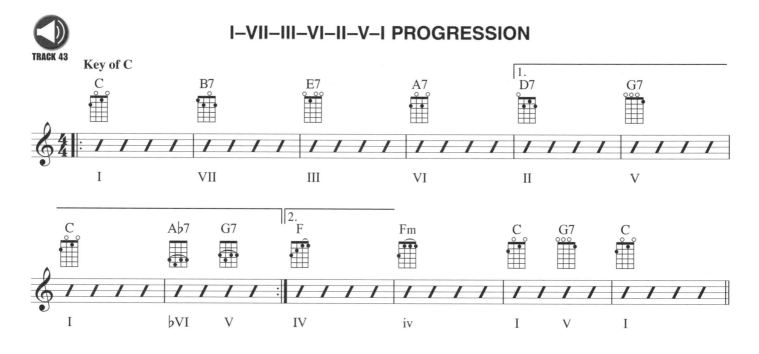

There's a standard, eight-bar circle-of-fifths ending that appears in countless songs, including "All of Me," "I'm Gonna Sit Right Down and Write Myself a Letter," "Pennies from Heaven," "Paper Doll," "(I'd Like to Get You on a) Slow Boat to China," "Who's Sorry Now," "Mona Lisa," "It's a Sin to Tell a Lie," and more. Sing one of these eight-bar endings while strumming:

STANDARD EIGHT-BAR ENDING

Play and analyze these two old jazz standards, which contain mostly circle-of-fifths chord movement. Strum and sing them along with the recording. Then study the progressions in terms of intervals, noticing VI–II–V–I's and other patterns, and try playing them in other keys. (The Roman numerals between the music and grids are there to help you identify the chords in terms of intervals and to understand chord movement.)

I USED TO LOVE YOU (BUT IT'S ALL OVER NOW)

FOR ME AND MY GAL

Make sure you can play typical circle-of-fifths-type chord changes, such as ii–V–I and I–vi–ii–V, in any key. These progressions occur in so many songs that it's important to memorize automatic, moveable ways of playing them. Strum these samples:

ii–V–I and I–vi–ii–V PROGRESSIONS

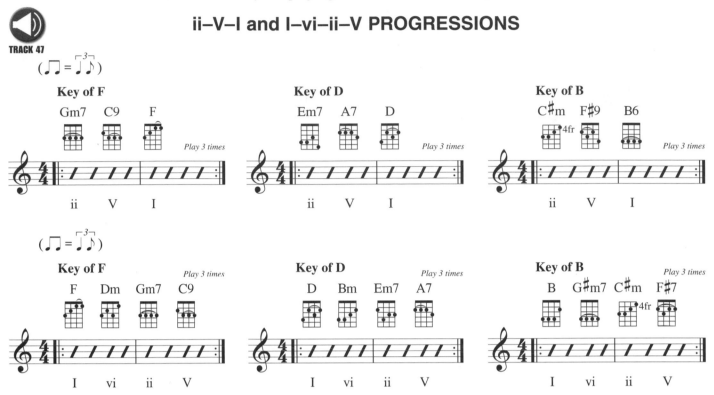

I–V–vi–IV is a more contemporary pop progression used in countless hits, as demonstrated in the Axis of Awesome's famous "4 Chord Song" YouTube video. Play this progression (written below in the key of C), and you can hum along with songs like "Don't Stop Believin'" (Journey), "You're Beautiful" (James Blunt), "I'm Yours" (Jason Mraz), "Can You Feel the Love Tonight" (Elton John), and "With or Without You" (U2). The four-chord sequence is not the whole song, but the main part of it:

If you double it up and play two chords per bar, it fits "Under the Bridge" (Red Hot Chili Peppers), "No Woman, No Cry" (Bob Marley), "Take on Me" (A-ha), and many more:

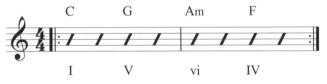

SUMMING UP—NOW YOU KNOW...

1. How to play several circle-of-fifths progressions in any key, including "Rhythm Changes."

2. How to automatically find the relative minor of any moveable major chord.

3. How to automatically find the chord that is a 4th above any moveable major chord.

4. The meaning of these musical terms:

   a) Relative Minor
   b) Relative Major
   c) Chromatic
   d) Bridge, "I Got Rhythm bridge"
   e) Rhythm Changes
   f) Standard Changes

THREE MOVEABLE BLUES BOXES
(MINOR PENTATONIC SCALES)

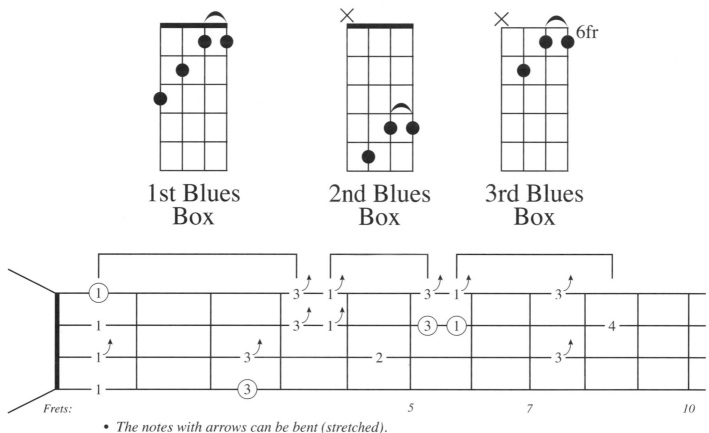

1st Blues Box   2nd Blues Box   3rd Blues Box

- *The notes with arrows can be bent (stretched).*
- *Each chord grid shows how to get your fretting hand "in position" for a blues box.*

WHY? The moveable scales of **ROADMAP #12**, often called *blues boxes*, are an invaluable tool for improvising single-note solos in nearly any popular music, including blues, rock, country, and jazz.

WHAT? **The three blues boxes above are F blues scales.** The root notes are circled. The numbers indicate suggested fingering positions.

Often, you can solo in one blues box throughout a song. Like the moveable major scales, blues boxes make it unnecessary to change scales with each chord change.

The blues boxes are pentatonic, which means they contain five notes. However, you can add other notes and still sound bluesy. The five notes are a good starting point.

HOW? To put your left hand in position for the first blues box, play an F formation at the appropriate fret. For the key of F, play the F formation at the 1st fret, which is an F chord. In other words, to play the first blues box, *find the key (root) note on the 1st string and fret it with your index finger.*

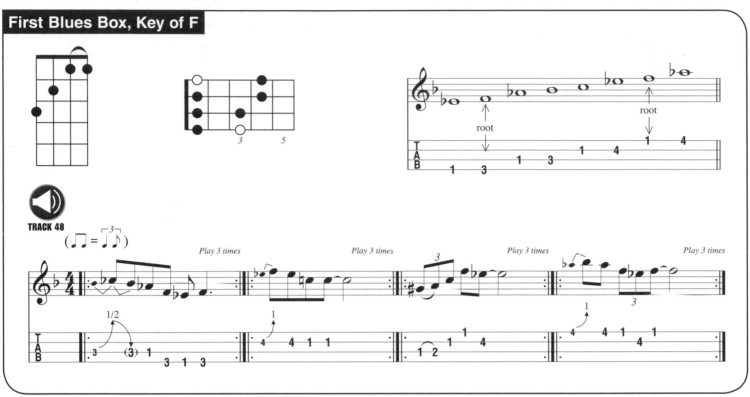

First Blues Box, Key of F

To put your left hand in position for the second blues box, play the first blues box and slide your index and middle fingers (on the 2nd and 3rd strings) up three frets. In F, play the F formation at the 1st fret and then slide up the 2nd and 3rd strings to the 4th and 5th frets, respectively. Notice that the root note (F, in the example below) is played on the 2nd string by your ring finger:

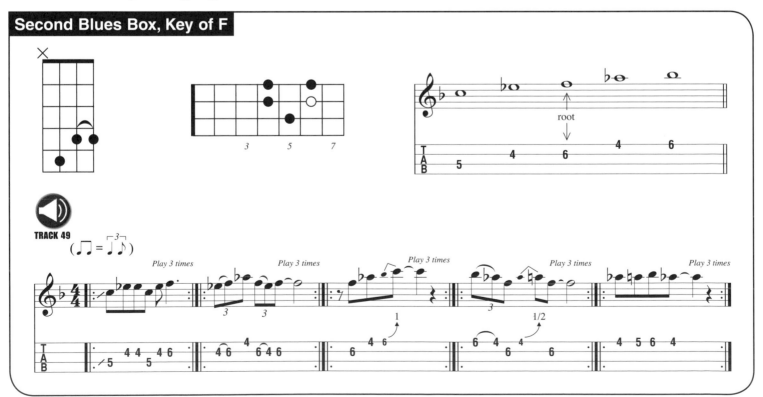

Second Blues Box, Key of F

68

To put your left hand in position for the third blues box, play the F formation of the IV chord. In the key of F, the IV chord is B♭, so fret the **F formation** at the 6th fret.

You can always play the IV chord by moving the I chord up five frets:

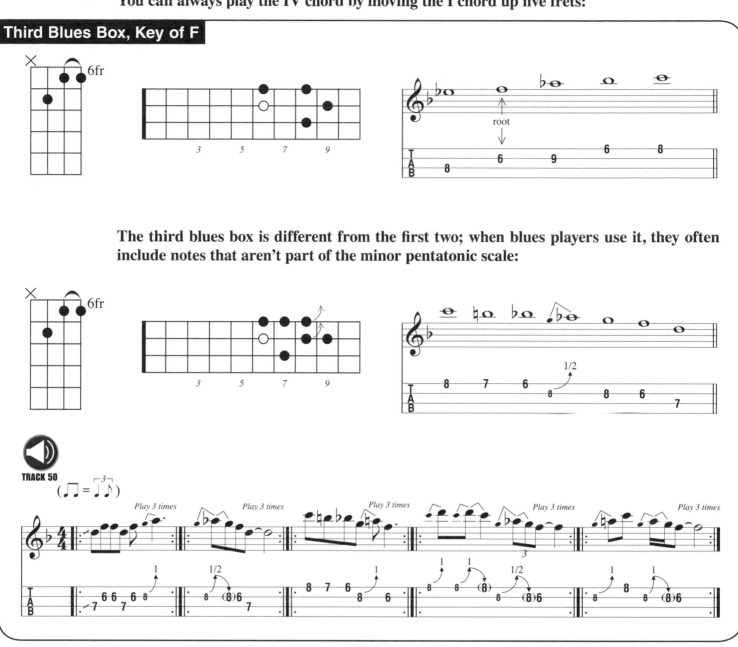

The third blues box is different from the first two; when blues players use it, they often include notes that aren't part of the minor pentatonic scale:

DO IT! **Use the blues boxes to solo on bluesy tunes.** In addition to blues tunes, that includes many rock, pop, country, and jazz songs—any song whose melody is based on the blues scale. If you play blues-scale-based licks over a tune, your ear will tell you immediately whether or not they sound appropriate.

The following solo illustrates the use of all three key-of-F blues boxes in a typical, jazzy 12-bar blues tune. It has the same flavor as "Route 66."

Notice that the F blues box licks work during the chord changes. This is one of the beauties of blues-box soloing: you don't have to change scales with the chord changes—one scale fits the whole tune.

SOME OTHER ROUTE

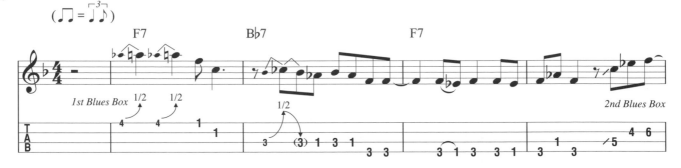

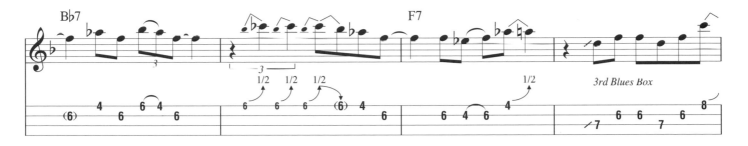

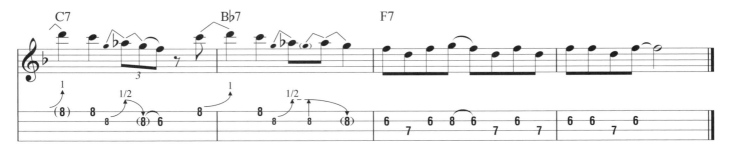

In case you want to join a rock jam session, here's a typical garage band chord progression in the key of E. The solo below uses all three E blues boxes. Since it's in E, the first box includes some open strings (it's what you get when you move the first F blues box down a fret).

1st Blues Box, Key of F   **1st Blues Box, Key of E**

GARAGE BAND ROCK

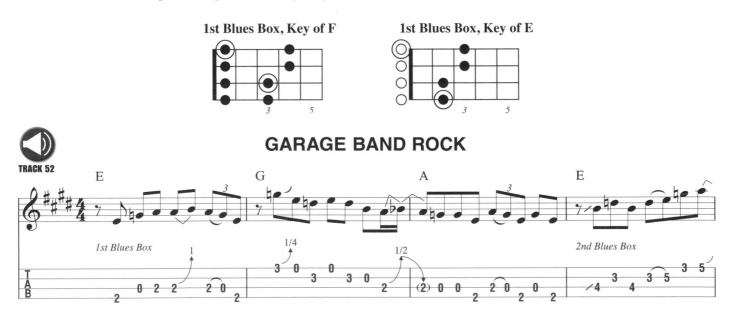

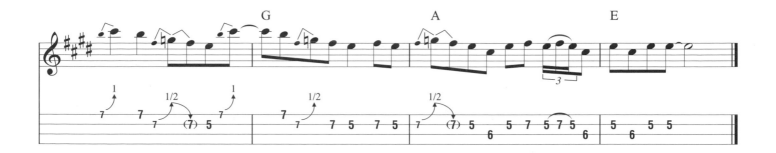

Blues-box soloing, especially the first two blues boxes, works on tunes that are in a minor key. Here's a bluesy solo to an old minor-key folk song in the key of G minor. It makes use of the first and second blues box.

WAYFARING STRANGER

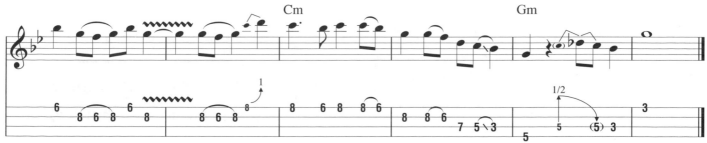

In some keys, if you try to use blues-box soloing, you quickly run out of frets. For example, if you play "Garage Band Rock" in D, the first blues box is up at the 10th fret, and higher blues boxes are impractical on the bari. But you can play the second and third boxes *an octave lower* (12 frets lower), like this:

2nd Blues Box, Key of D   **3rd Blues Box, Key of D**

GARAGE BAND ROCK—Key of D

TRACK 54

Often, the third blues box works well in non-bluesy tunes, where the first and second boxes sound inappropriate. "On the Beach at Waikiki," below, is about as far from a blues as you can get. It's in the key of G, and the solo consists of G licks in the third blues box.

ON THE BEACH AT WAIKIKI

TRACK 55

Relative minor blues scale substitution: When a song does not have a bluesy feel, you can still use the first and second blues boxes; just play them *three frets lower than the song's actual key.* For example, the following version of "The World Is Waiting for the Sunrise" is in the key of C, but the solo makes use of the first and second *A blues boxes.*

THE WORLD IS WAITING FOR THE SUNRISE

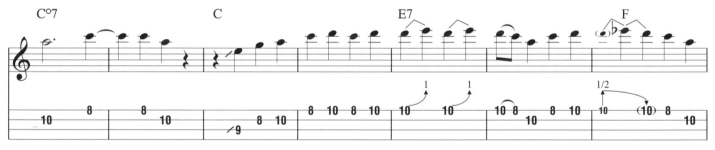

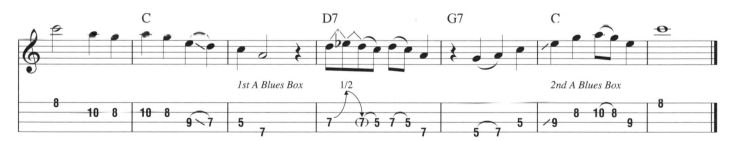

SUMMING UP—NOW YOU KNOW...

1. Three moveable blues boxes.
2. Many licks that go with each box.
3. How to use the boxes to improvise single-note solos in any key.
4. How to substitute the relative minor blues scale when blues boxes don't fit in a tune.

USING THE PRACTICE TRACKS

The **ROADMAPS** in this book illustrate many backup and soloing styles, including:

- Strumming or picking many voicings of any one chord.

- Playing chord families "automatically."

- Single-note soloing based on moveable and first-position major scales.

- Single-note soloing based on blues boxes.

- Playing circle-of-fifths progressions "automatically."

On the four practice tracks, the bari is separated from the rest of the band—it's on the right side of the audio mix. You can tune it out and use the band as backup, trying out any soloing techniques you like. You can also imitate the recorded bari parts. When you access the audio online for this book, you can use the *PLAYBACK+* audio player to pan the mix to either side for optimum practice. Here are the soloing and backup ideas for each track:

#1 FRANKIE AND JOHNNY (in E, A, D, G, C, and F, in that order)

TRACK 57

This slightly altered, 12-bar blues is played six times, in six different keys. The bari is featured alone on the right side of the audio mix and uses the first-position major scale of each key to play the melody, with some embellishment. On the left side of the mix, the bari strums rhythm with a small band. Here are a few practice ideas:

1. Play the melody in all keys, using first-position scales and adding some embellishments.

2. Ad-lib single-note solos, using first-position and moveable scales.

3. Strum the rhythm, using first-position chords and then moveable chords. Either way, you're practicing using I–IV–V chord families. Here's the 12-bar blues progression:

$$\frac{4}{4} \| I \ V \ | \ I \ | \ I \ V \ | \ I \ | \ IV \ | \ \% \ | \ \% \ | \ I \ | \ V \ | \ \% \ | \ I \ | \ \% \ \|$$

#2 DOWN BY THE RIVERSIDE (in G)

TRACK 58

The track goes around this old gospel tune twice.

Verse: $\frac{4}{4}$ G | % | % | % | D7 | % | G | % | % | % | % | % | D7 | % | G | G7 ‖
           I   V   I   V   I

Chorus: ‖: C | % | G | % | D7 | % | G | % :‖
          IV   I   V   I

Use this track to practice **ROADMAP #6** (the **F–D–B ROADMAP**). The song stays on one chord for several bars at a time, so you can shift from one voicing to another as you strum backup. For example, at the beginning of the tune, strum the F formation at the 3rd fret for one bar, then the D formation at the 7th fret for one bar, then the B formation at the 10th fret for a bar, and so on.

#3 SOME OTHER ROUTE (in A and D)

TRACK 59

The bari plays blues scales throughout this 12-bar blues. Using the chords below, you can practice strumming along, then practice your blues licks. The first two times around the tune, in the key of A, the bari's solo is based on the first and second A blues boxes. The third and fourth times around, the song is in D, and the bari's solo makes use of the first and second B blues boxes. Those are substitute blues boxes, three frets below the D blues boxes. (B is the relative minor of D major.)

Key of A:

$\frac{4}{4}$‖: A7 | D9 | A7 | ⁒ | D9 | ⁒ | A7 | ⁒ | E9 | D9 | A7 | E9 :‖
      I   IV   I   IV   I   V   IV   I   V

Key of D:

$\frac{4}{4}$‖: D9 | G7 | D9 | ⁒ | G7 | ⁒ | D9 | ⁒ | A7 | G7 | D9 | A7 :‖
      I   IV   I   IV   I   V   IV   I   V

#4 TAKE ME OUT TO THE BALL GAME (in D and G)

TRACK 60

Use this classic tune to practice circle-of-fifths-type chord changes. Play it with first-position chords, then try it with as many moveable chords as possible. Here are the chord changes in both keys. Intervals (Roman numerals) are written below the chord names to help you be aware of the VI–II–V–I progressions. Also notice the classic eight-bar ending that begins on the IV chord, as mentioned in the circle-of-fifths chapter (**ROADMAP #11**). **Note:** In this variation of the eight-bar ending, #iv° (C#°7, in the key of G) is played instead of iv (Cm).

Key of D:

$\frac{3}{4}$‖: D | ⁒ | A7 | ⁒ | D | ⁒ | A7 | ⁒ | B7 | ⁒ | Em | ⁒ | E7 | ⁒ | A7 | ⁒ |
      I   V   I   V   VI   ii   II   V

| D | ⁒ | A7 | ⁒ | D7 | ⁒ | G | ⁒ | ⁒ | G#°7 | D | B7 | E7 | A7 | D | ⁒ :‖
  I   V   I   IV   #iv°   I   VI   II   V   I

Key of G:

$\frac{3}{4}$‖: G | ⁒ | D7 | ⁒ | G | ⁒ | D7 | ⁒ | E7 | ⁒ | Am | ⁒ | A7 | ⁒ | D7 | ⁒ |
      I   V   I   V   VI   ii   II   V

| G | ⁒ | D7 | ⁒ | G7 | ⁒ | C | ⁒ | ⁒ | C#°7 | G | E7 | A7 | D7 | G | ⁒ :‖
  I   V   I   IV   #iv°   I   VI   II   V   I

CHORD DICTIONARY

MOVEABLE CHORDS

This chord dictionary offers several different moveable chord formations for each chord type. The chord shapes can all be found in Chapters 3, 4, and 5, but this format makes them easier to find. The root of each formation is circled, so if you know where the notes are located up and down the fretboard, you can play any chord several different ways. If the root is not included in the formation, a blank circle is written, indicating where the root is in relation to the chord shape. (Don't play those blank circles; they are just there to show you where to place the chord on the fretboard.) The interval formula is written for each chord type (e.g., major chord = 1–3–5).

That brings up an interesting question: with only four notes per chord on the bari, how can you adequately express subtle chords like 13ths or 11ths? The answer is that you have to pick the most important notes in the chord formula and skip the rest. Here are some tips:

1. Often, the root is expendable, as is the 5th.

2. If the chord is a seventh, the flatted 7th note must be included.

3. You also need the 3rd to make the minor or major part of the chord audible.

4. The "upper" intervals of a chord are essential. For example, if a chord is a 9th, 11th, or 13th, it will only sound like its namesake if it contains that high note (i.e., the 9th, 11th, or 13th).

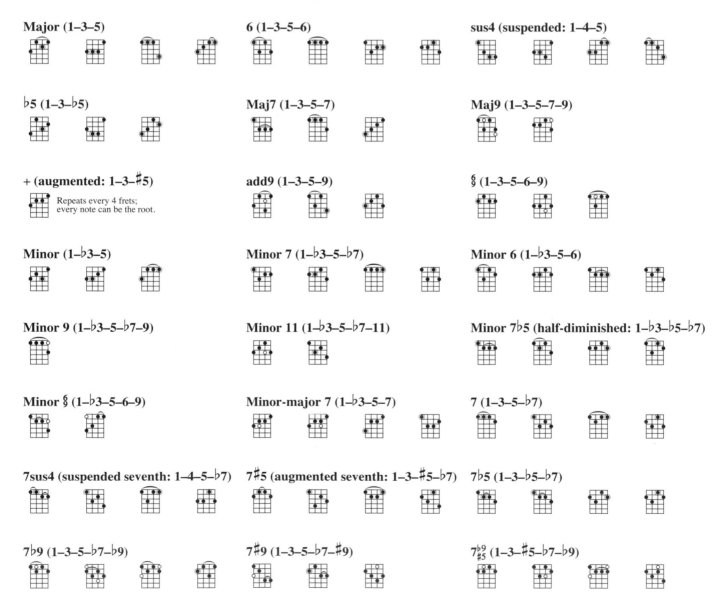

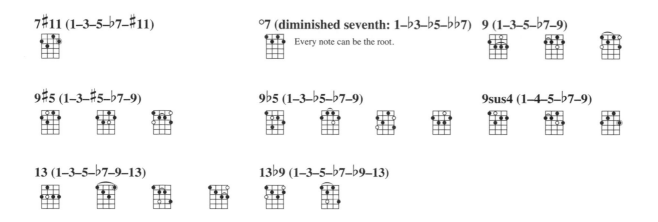

7#11 (1–3–5–♭7–#11)

°7 (diminished seventh: 1–♭3–♭5–♭♭7)
Every note can be the root.

9 (1–3–5–♭7–9)

9#5 (1–3–#5–♭7–9)

9♭5 (1–3–♭5–♭7–9)

9sus4 (1–4–5–♭7–9)

13 (1–3–5–♭7–9–13)

13♭9 (1–3–5–♭7–♭9–13)

FIRST-POSITION CHORDS

Here are the first-position chords (chords that include open strings and are therefore not moveable) used in this book. Many of them are related to moveable chords. For example, if you move the first-position A up a fret, you have to raise the open E (1st string) by a fret, as well. The result is the moveable B chord formation.

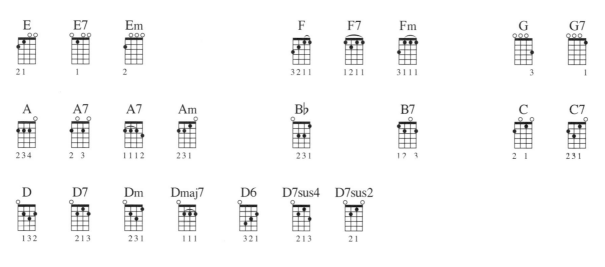

ABOUT THE AUTHOR

Fred Sokolow is best known as the author of over 150 instructional and transcription books and DVDs for guitar, mandolin, banjo, ukulele, Dobro, and lap steel. Fred has long been a well-known West Coast multi-string performer and recording artist, particularly on the acoustic music scene. He is often featured as a performer and teacher at ukulele, banjo, and guitar festivals all over the world. The diverse musical genres covered in his books and DVDs, along with several bluegrass, jazz, and rock CDs he has released, demonstrate his mastery of many musical styles. Whether he's playing Delta bottleneck blues, bluegrass, traditional Hawaiian uke, or old-time banjo, '30s swing guitar, or screaming rock solos, he does it with authenticity and passion.

Fred's ukulele and guitar books include:

- *Fretboard Roadmaps for Ukulele*, book/audio (with Jim Beloff), Hal Leonard
- *101 Ukulele Tips*, book/audio (with Ronny Schiff), Hal Leonard
- *Fretboard Roadmaps for Guitar*, book/audio, Hal Leonard
- *Fingerstyle Ukulele*, book/audio, Hal Leonard
- *Slide and Slack Key Ukulele*, book/audio, Hal Leonard
- *Blues Ukulele*, book/audio, Flea Market Music, distributed by Hal Leonard
- *Bluegrass Ukulele*, book/audio, Flea Market Music, distributed by Hal Leonard

Contact Fred with any questions about this book or any of his other titles at: Sokolowmusic.com.

TRACK LIST/SONG INDEX

BARITONE UKULELE NOTATION LEGEND

THE MUSICAL STAFF shows pitches and rhythms and is divided by bar lines into measures. Pitches are named after the first seven letters of the alphabet.

TABLATURE graphically represents the ukulele fingerboard. Each horizontal line represents a a string, and each number represents a fret.

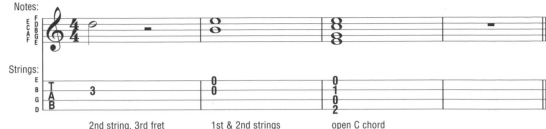

2nd string, 3rd fret   1st & 2nd strings open, played together   open C chord

HALF-STEP BEND: Strike the note and bend up 1/2 step.

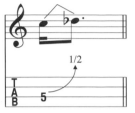

WHOLE-STEP BEND: Strike the note and bend up one step.

GRACE NOTE BEND: Strike the note and immediately bend up as indicated.

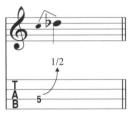

SLIGHT (MICROTONE) BEND: Strike the note and bend up 1/4 step.

BEND AND RELEASE: Strike the note and bend up as indicated, then release back to the original note. Only the first note is struck.

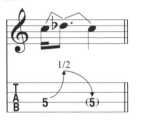

PRE-BEND: Bend the note as indicated, then strike it.

VIBRATO: The string is vibrated by rapidly bending and releasing the note with the fretting hand.

HAMMER-ON: Strike the first (lower) note with one finger, then sound the higher note (on the same string) with another finger by fretting it without picking.

PULL-OFF: Place both fingers on the notes to be sounded. Strike the first note and without picking, pull the finger off to sound the second (lower) note.

LEGATO SLIDE: Strike the first note and then slide the same fret-hand finger up or down to the second note. The second note is not struck.

SHIFT SLIDE: Same as legato slide, except the second note is struck.

TRILL: Very rapidly alternate between the notes indicated by continuously hammering on and pulling off.

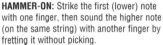

TREMOLO PICKING: The note is picked as rapidly and continuously as possible.

NOTE: Tablature numbers in parentheses mean:

1. The note is being sustained over a system (note in standard notation is tied), or

2. The note is sustained, but a new articulation (such as a hammer-on, pull-off, slide or vibrato) begins, or

3. The note is a barely audible "ghost" note (note in standard notation is also in parentheses).

Additional Musical Definitions

(accent)	• Accentuate note (play it louder)
(staccato)	• Play the note short
D.S. al Coda	• Go back to the sign (𝄋), then play until the measure marked "*To Coda*," then skip to the section labelled "**Coda**."
D.C. al Fine	• Go back to the beginning of the song and play until the measure marked "*Fine*" (end).
N.C.	• No chord.
	• Repeat measures between signs.
1. 2.	• When a repeated section has different endings, play the first ending only the first time and the second ending only the second time.

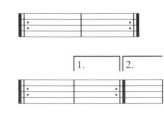

80